STRE [illegible] ELF

STRETCH YOURSELF

How to Create Your Dream Life

VICKRANT MAHAJAN

Word Smith

First published in 2009 by WordSmith

WordSmith

E-mail: wordsmithbooks@gmail.com
ISBN 81-87909-15-3

Typeset by
Mindways Design
1410 Chiranjiv Tower
43 Nehru Place
New Delhi 110019

Printed and bound in India by
Syndicate Binders
A-20 Hosiery Complex
Noida 201305

To God,
the light of my life

"The more you are, the more you can become, and the more you can become, the more you can yet be."

— Neale Donald Walsch

Contents

Acknowledgements

Let me acknowledge, first and foremost, that I am merely a conduit for this book. It contains wisdom of the ages (the way I understand it), passed from innumerable enlightened souls. In my quest for evolution, I have had the good fortune of benefiting from the timeless experience of countless people who have inspired or taught me generously about the power of stretching. I bow down in deep gratitude before them:

My soulmate and best friend, Ronicka, for stretching my definition of love and togetherness, and for teaching me what true acceptance means. She is God's truest blessing to me.

My parents, Veenaa and Sham Kishor Gupta, for stretching their vision and resources for me always. Thanks Ma and Pa, especially, for showing me how to dream big.

My sister, Niddhi, for the purity of her soul and the simplicity of her heart, and my brother-in-law, Vinod, for his ever-resilient nature.

My father-in-law, Avtar Singh Kandhari, for exemplifying how to stretch oneself incessantly in the pursuit of one's dreams.

My nephews, Aryan, Arnav and Prabhmann, for continually stretching the child in me.

Vipan Sharma bhaiya, for his priceless insights and nuggets of wisdom. It is thanks to him and those magical two words of his that I got the idea for this book.

Punam didi, for stretching the generosity of her spirit and warmth of her being always.

Sapnnaa Kapoor, for her unceasing zest for work and for stretching the true meaning of friendship for me.

Buddha, Krishna, Guru Nanak, Christ and Kabir, for making me whatever I am today or will ever be.

Baba Brahmadev, for ever so subtly yet surely stretching my definition of faith and spirituality.

Paramhansa Yogananda, Swami Vivekananda, Mahatma Gandhi, Guru Ding Le Mei, Mother Teresa, Robert H Schuller, Neale Donald Walsch, Ralph Waldo Emerson, Osho, Yogi Ashok, Sri Sri Ravi Shankar, Henry David Thoreau, Napoleon Hill, Dale Carnegie, Zig Ziglar, Deepak Chopra, Robin Sharma, Dr Wayne W Dyer, Rhonda Byrne, Dada Vaswani, Linda Goodman, Eckhart Tolle, Norman Vincent Peale, Cheiro, Rumi, and many other enlightened ones, for perpetually stretching and deepening my understanding of life.

Hrithik Roshan, for having such an implicit faith in this project — thank you so much, Hrithik, for teaching me so wonderfully why you are what you are.

Simran Singh and Afsar Zaidi, for stretching every realm of possibility and for carving my cherished dream to life — a *big* thank you, Carving Dreams.

And to that one friend: I owe it to you for stretching me out of mediocrity. But for you, I wouldn't have known the extraordinary.

Above all, to God, the very essence of my life. Every moment, I surrender myself to you totally and allow you to mould me like only you can.

Thank you all.

Introduction

A philosopher once said: "The scope of our lives is far greater than our biggest imagination!" According to research, most of us consciously use only 10 per cent of our brainpower. Even geniuses like Edison and Einstein purportedly used less than 20 per cent of their full endowment. So you can just imagine the sheer plethora of human potential that's still untapped and the humongous scope that one can stretch oneself to.

We human beings epitomise the principle of stretching by virtue of our very existence: from a tiny atom infinitely smaller than a pinpoint, we evolve into full-grown humans, five, six, seven or eight feet tall! Nature converts a tiny seed into an entire orchard! A single 1-rupee coin has mass sufficient enough to be converted into energy that can light up the entire city of New Delhi for a few hours! A moment stretches into a minute, an hour, a day, a week, a month, a year, a decade, a century, a millennium and eventually into eternity! Every form of matter in the universe is a tribute to the stretching process. The universe itself — originating from a primordial mass of matter, still expanding after 13.7 billion years — is the archetype of the power of stretching.

There are individuals galore who have proven the merit of stretching in every age and generation. Abraham Lincoln stretched himself to be the president of the United States in the light of a lamp post, and after seven unsuccessful political tries! Edison's resilience is legendary: he stretched himself over 10,000 experiments (or so-called failures) before creating the light bulb! Helen Keller, even after being deaf, dumb and mute, stretched herself — and in the process the threshold of the major physical faculties in a human — to learn 5 languages and write 12 books! Andrew Carnegie stretched himself out of abject poverty and selling newspapers on the pavements to be the richest man of his time! Bill Gates stretched himself out of being a college dropout to creating one of the biggest corporate empires in the world — not just that, he then stretched himself out of corporate apathy and avarice into becoming one of the greatest philanthropists of all time! Lance Armstrong stretched himself out of life-threatening cancer to win the Tour de France a world-record seven consecutive times! JK Rowling stretched herself out of being a single unemployed mother to the first-ever billionaire writer in history! Sunil Bharti Mittal stretched his borrowed capital of Rs 20,000 into a net worth of Rs 60,000 crore, and still counting! Oprah Winfery stretched herself from grinding poverty, and wearing dresses made out of potato sacks, to a stature so high that *Time* magazine eulogised her "the most influential woman in the world", and she became the first-ever black billionaire in history! These are just a few of the known instances — if you look around among your family, friends, acquaintances or neighbours, you'd find scores of instances that attest to the power of stretching in some way or the other.

It's not just individuals but countries and cities too that abundantly benefit from the power of stretching themselves. Dubai and Singapore are classic examples. The former was a desert wilderness and the latter a fledgling impoverished colony till 40 years ago! Both countries were dependant on the outside world for even basic necessities like food and water. Today, they have sidestepped their natural limitations and grown phenomenally to create the best standards of living in the world. Japan has been repeatedly devastated by natural calamities, yet today it has one of the best economies in the world. Europe was completely ravaged by World War II yet look where it is today! The Emirates are a classic example of what you can do with stretching yourself, even in a desert — today they have the Louvre, Formula One, Christie's, the tallest building in the world, the maximum number of skyscrapers! Likewise with Las Vegas, the most alluring megapolis on the face of our planet. Look at its glittering casinos and luxury hotels — all created in the middle of nowhere! The China story is yet another testament to the power of stretching. A country that started participating in the Olympics only in 1984 (after a boycott) suddenly emerged as the topmost gold-medal winners in the world at the 2008 Olympics — all within 25 years! How? By the power of proactive stretching. As for their economic story, the result is there for the world to see!

If you notice, most people "hide their lights under a bushel", as the proverb goes. They leash themselves up too much. Already, the time at every person's disposal is a predetermined 24 hours — no matter who one is or what one does, no one can have more than 24 hours! In that stipulated time frame also, if one doesn't stretch oneself, then one is accepting limitation as the leitmotif of life. Whatever you do, don't be one of those who live and die with "their music still unplayed". Go out there and play out your music. And that will happen only when you stretch yourself.

Having said that, one must emphasise that stretching yourself doesn't imply burning yourself out. There is a fine line between the two. When you stretch yourself, you do it in accordance with the holistic equilibrium of your body, mind and soul, rather than singularly. Stretching yourself doesn't imply that you deprive yourself of rest or sleep, nor does it imply burning the candle at both ends. Rather, igniting it at one end is good enough — provided you ignite it properly!

Once you initiate the right moves by stretching yourself, your life automatically snowballs into bigger, better and higher realms by the day. As Robert H Schuller has said: "Once success starts, it can never stop. For success is never-ending. Even the setting of the sun does not mark an end to the day that is past, for that day is given eternal life as it becomes a part of irrevocable history." So let your success and your life truly start. For once it does, it will never end. Stretch yourself in every area of your life. Make every stopping stone your stepping stone. Stretching yourself will eventually result in a startling renaissance, a complete makeover for your entire life, with incalculable paybacks and dividends.

In the ensuing seven chapters, you will rediscover how to max life at every level: mental, physical, spiritual, financial, human, professional and personal. Let me state that it is by no means a gospel of truth or how it *must* be done — rather it is just a gist of my observations and insights, and how it could be realistically done. *Stretch Yourself* is an amalgam of all the techniques that have helped me incredibly in my life: whether it was at the Grasim Mr India 2003 pageant, in establishing my wife Ronicka and me as one of the most unique photographer couples in Asia, or in my numerology consultations for over 15,000 people till date. So I have taken it upon myself to pass on the essence of my learnings to you. As you peruse the following pages you might agree with me or not, but my only request to you would be to keep an open mind and a willing heart.

Neale Donald Walsch has beautifully said in *Conversations with God*: "There is only purpose for all of life, and that's for you and all that lives to experience *fullest* glory. The wonder of this purpose is that it is never-ending. An ending is a limitation, and God's purpose is without such a boundary. Should there come such a moment in which you experience yourself in your fullest glory, you will in that instant imagine an even greater glory to fulfil." So imagine the greatest glory that you can and give it all that you've got.

If you look at it, it's you alone that are thrusting yourself and you alone that are holding yourself back. Nothing else. The onus for your life and your success lies solely on you. Period. As they say: "A mountain can't get any bigger — but you can!" So stretch yourself, make yourself bigger than any mountain you encounter and create the life of your dreams, like only you can.

Chapter One

MENTALLY

"As is your sort of mind, so is your sort of search —
you'll find what you desire."

— Robert Browning

1

Think BLOCKBUSTER

Disraeli once said: "Life is too short to be little!"

It should be your constant and foremost endeavour to live the grandest vision of yourself, to strive for the biggest scale you can conceive. Most people relegate themselves to small-mindedness, with a barely-get-by mentality. They settle for too little: "If I just get a 10 per cent raise, I will be happy" or "If I just get the next Saturday off, I will be glad". They never imagine or ordain a 100 per cent (or a 1,000 per cent) jump, or a month off, and no prizes for guessing — they never get it! Because, like Ralph Waldo Emerson said: "The ancestor of every action is a thought!"

Most of humanity is stuck in a straitjacket, thinking it has reached its limits. Way too many people accept a status quo in their lives and keep dredging on. They never stretch their faith, potential or thoughts for anything bigger. But actually it is human destiny to constantly be bigger, better and higher than ever before. Aren't we so much more evolved than Homo Sapiens from 2,00,000 years ago? Could people live in a temperature-controlled environment even 100 years ago? Fly to wherever they wanted to go? See "live" an event happening thousands of miles away? Call anyone from anywhere? Zip around in the swankiest cars and go from 0 to 100 kph in 4 seconds? Have access to untold information at the click of a button? Have limb, rather heart, transplants? Shoot and save thousands of pictures on a small stamp-sized memory card without the aid of photographic film? Shop at 24-hour stores? See a movie on a phone? Replace money with plastic? Land man on the moon and send satellites to Mars and the farthest orbits of the universe? Clone livestock and be on the verge of cloning a human?

All this happened because some people believed in the power of the human mind to shape the future. They had a vision and pursued it doggedly. They stretched the boundaries of imagination, of possibility, and gave birth to a manifest reality. Likewise, we all can birth a beautiful future of mankind, and an equally wonderful present, if we start thinking beyond what is to what *can* be. All we have to do to accomplish that promise is to step out of our little boxes and start doing some big thinking.

Napoleon Hill once wonderfully said: "There are no limitations to the mind, except those that we acknowledge!" If you think you can do something, or if you think you can't, the barrier is solely in your mind.

Miles Hilton-Barber, the first blind man ever to fly halfway across the world and to run the "toughest foot-race on earth", the 150-mile long Marathon des Sables, once famously said: "Your success lies within a distance of about five inches between your ears!"

Katsusuke Yanagisawa stretched every known barrier of biological age when he climbed Mount Everest at the age of 71! When he was asked later how he did it, he said: "People had been telling me all along why it was impossible. I just kept thinking why it was possible!" That's how simple — and powerful — the magic of big thinking is! When faced with it, even the mightiest mountain stands humbled.

Donald Trump once said: "To be successful, you have to separate yourself from 98 per cent of the rest of the world. Sure, you can get into that special 2 per cent at the top, and it is not just by being smart, working hard and investing wisely. There is a formula, a recipe for success that the top 2 per cent live by, and that you too can follow to be successful. It is: Think Big and Kick Ass!"

Warren Buffet, the world's most successful investor ever, was turned down by Harvard Business School, was rejected by his first employer even when he offered his services for free and abjectly failed in his first commercial investment! But by dint of one magic talisman, he turned his fortunes around and became the wealthiest man in the world. His talisman was: "Think big and proclaim success beyond failure!"

Dhirubhai Ambani — who went from selling pakoras to pilgrims in Mount Girnar over the weekends and working as a gas-station attendant in Yemen to creating one of the biggest corporate empires Asia has ever seen — had one abiding mantra in life: "Think big, think fast, think ahead!"

If you consider it, one has to think anyway. It's not like those who don't think big, don't think at all! There is not a single person in this world who doesn't think. My point is: if you're going to think anyway, then why not think BIG!

Napoleon Hill once observed: "No more effort is required to aim high in life than is required to accept misery and poverty!" All it takes is an initiative, a resolve that you're going to have a mega thinking, come what may. It is as simple as choosing to eat between a burger and a fruit. You can eat either. You just have to decide which one you want.

Our mind is a wonderful buffet of thoughts. The onus is on us to pick up our plate and fill it with what we want. All it takes is a choice — a personal pact to live our life at the grandest mode possible. And no matter what your present level of thinking, it's never too late to reconfigure. As Tennyson has said: "Come my friends, 'tis not too late to seek a newer world." So come, let's think blockbuster and create a world that nobody before us has even dreamt of!

2

Be an Idea Miner

Robert H Schuller once said: "Nobody has a money problem. People only have an idea problem. So long as you have the right idea, money will never be a problem." And it's so true! Microsoft started with an idea, Reliance started with an idea, and so did Pepsi, McDonald's, GE, Wal-Mart, Wipro and countless other conglomerates. Likewise, *The Fountainhead, My Fair Lady, Catch-22, Guide, Ulysses, Gone with the Wind* and all literature manifested from an idea. Ditto for *Titanic, Life is Beautiful, Citizen Kane, Gladiator, Dilwale Dulhaniya Le Jayenge* and all the movies ever made. Every television or radio program started with an idea. Every institution birthed from an idea, as did every philosophy. Every mode of transport — airplane, bus, car, train, cycle, boat, skate — owes its origin to an idea. Look around, and any piece of furniture, cutlery, decoration, any item of utility ever made or being used, started with an idea. Same with every sport and mode of recreation. So, what's the bottom line? If you want to do anything worthwhile, start harvesting ideas.

There's an infinity of ideas waiting to be tapped into. I once read this memorable quote somewhere: "Champions are not blue-sky dreamers or intellectual giants — rather, they are idea miners!" Bill Gates, when asked the secret behind his success, said: "We have a brilliant team that comes to work every morning with *ideas* of creating something better."

Ideas are veritable money machines. This story illustrates it best: Years ago, Sabeer Bhatia and Jack Smith wanted to start a company and had been brainstorming possible business ideas for a month. They wanted to e-mail each other notes but were afraid that their bosses at Apple Computers might glean their e-mail that was on their office network and accuse them of spending their working hours on personal projects. Frustrated by this problem, they came up with a unique idea: free e-mail accounts that could be accessed anonymously over the Web. Consequently Hotmail was born — the rest, as they say, is an oft-repeated rags-to-riches legend!

If you carefully observe, everything in the universe starts with an idea, and then develops into a tangible reality. Just come up with the right idea, and the world is waiting to lap it up. One idea can, and does, change the course of an entire life. Sometimes you consciously birth it, and sometimes it strikes you like a bolt from the blue. The train on which JK Rowling was travelling from Manchester to London got delayed by few hours. To utilise the spare time, she started doodling on a piece of paper. Soon "out of nowhere" she got the idea for the story of a young boy attending a school of wizardry — and Harry Potter was born! Likewise, Sylvester Stallone got the idea for *Rocky* while watching a news clip about a boxing match between Muhammad Ali and Chuck Wepner, and wrote the script within three days! Similarly, Jaideep Sahni got the idea for *Chak De India* from a newspaper story about the Indian women's hockey team winning the gold medal at the 2002 Commonwealth Games. As Po Brosnan once said: "Anybody can have an idea. And the best ideas are right under your nose!"

Be open to new influences and make yourself a freewheeler who never shies away from new ideas. Set yourself a goal of coming up with at least one new idea a week for three months related to any aspect of your life. That's how Thomas Edison worked. He had a "personal idea quota" that involved coming up with the idea of one minor invention every ten days and one major invention every six months — no wonder, by the time he passed on, he held 1,093 patents, which is still the world record for any individual! Though you may find the process a little difficult initially, but as you progress, you will find that new ideas just keep snowballing. And don't be dismissive about their workability. Most people, as soon as they have ideas, throw them out of the window. They deem them improbable, unworkable, "not for us". But, actually if we look at it, every success has started when the receiver has accepted an idea (even if uninvited or bizarre) openly and embraced it as their own! That person was the one who did not dismiss it offhandedly as an impossibility but rather explored its possibility. They applied their mind to the prospect of turning that idea into a living reality. They were charged with excitement on being faced with a new concept. And they eventually became pioneers. A great visionary once said: "The beauty about ideas is they take on a life of their own, and live on long after the person who has birthed them has gone." So stretch your mind to birth dynamic, new ideas — who knows which one of them might give you the elixir of immortality!

3

Condition Your Mind Consciously

Someone has wonderfully said: "Success is an inside job." It means that we have to first conceive in our mind what we wish to receive on a tangible level and look beyond where we are to where we want to be. Let me share with you a real-life instance to show you how this works:

I know a girl, Swati, who was from Dehradun and had come to Delhi looking for a job. She had really hit the trough financially and had no money to pay her rent or phone bills. However, despite her bleak situation, she did not let the gravity of the situation affect her spirit. Even in that trying time, she did something extraordinary. She was very fond of shopping, and her favourite hangout was Select Citywalk, an upmarket shopping mall in South Delhi. She'd dress up in her best clothes, walk down two kilometres from her home to the mall (since she could not afford even an autorickshaw) and spend hours just gazing at the show windows of Calvin Klein, Tommy Hilfiger and Mango, and walk in confidently pretending to be a customer. She'd pick up the dresses she liked, take them to the trying room, preen herself in front of the mirror and then eventually put them aside on some pretext or the other. She kept telling herself that one day she'd be able to afford all those dresses. Interestingly, she did this at the most tumultuous phase of her life, when anybody lesser would not even have looked at the mall, let alone walk inside. When I asked her the rationale behind this unusual practice, she said something that impacted me very profoundly. She said: "I wanted to be in a place where I could stimulate my mind. I thought if I could be amid affluence often, my luck would change for the better." What an inspiring approach, I thought to myself! Twice a week, she'd go there unfailingly, no matter what — even if she didn't have money to eat. And, providentially, within three months, she got a very promising job in a multinational bank. Her financial woes dissipated, and she was soon buying — not just window-shopping — the brands she liked the most. Now, some would call this turnaround luck, but it'd be fair to attribute it to her pluck. She dared herself to be in the place where she really wanted to be, and the whole universe worked for her. As that line from *The Alchemist* so wonderfully says: "Plant the seeds in the universe, and the whole universe will conspire to get you what you want."

In his book *My Life in Tibet*, Guru Ding Le Mei tells us of Tibetan men sitting unclothed in sub-zero weather conditions for hour upon hour, and maintaining the entire body at such a feverish heat that snow around them is melted! They can live without perceptible breathing for a long time, slow their heart rate to almost zero and hold fierce wild animals at bay with just a glance! They make this possible through a technique called

"Tahumo" or conditioning the mind to attain mastery over the body — now *that's* how powerful mind power is!

You can either look at the sky and say "How dull it is!" or you can say "How vast it is!" It's all about conditioning and proactively training the mind. Change your frequency from self-pity to self-regard and then watch the magic unfold. For results to be solid and enduring, a complete restructuring of the mind has to take place. As someone has said: "Life is just a mirror, and the outside is a reflection of the inside." Once you hardware your inside for success, the outside is going to reflect that naturally. It's exactly how a computer works: if the software has become corrupted, all you have to do is reload it. Likewise, if a line of thinking is not working, all you have to do is reprogram your mind.

If your house is dirty, you cannot invite guests unless you first clean it. Likewise, if your prevailing thoughts are self-defeating, you cannot usher in change unless you clean up your mind first. As Johann Von Goethe said: "The moment one definitely commits oneself, providence moves too." As soon as you reconfigure your mind, all the cosmic forces get favourably aligned. Constantly inundate your mind with bright and happy thoughts, words and sensations, and that's exactly the shape your life will acquire. Train your mind to see the very best, and the very best shall come to pass. As William Blake said: "What is now proved was once only imagined!" So imagine the unimagined and make it your living reality.

4

Raise the Bar

Captain Cook once said: "I had ambition not only to go farther than any man had ever been before, but as far as it was possible for a man to go!" The problem with the greater proportion of humanity is not lack of talent, but the fact that it's content with too little. The reason most people make do with substandard is that they keep their parametres very low. On the other end of the spectrum, champions or world-class achievers are what they are because they set their personal standards very high. They push themselves not just on stray occasions, but at every given opportunity. To them, personal excellence is not by default but by design. In order to max our lives, we have to stretch ourselves beyond, and out of, mediocrity into the realm of excellence. True, excellence demands stringent personal commitment, but once one is accustomed to it, then one just cannot settle for anything less. If, for instance, you've beheld the beauty and splendour of a rare diamond, the sheen of faux crystals won't appeal to you. Likewise, if you've set yourself lofty standards, then quotidian mediocre standards won't enthral you. You'd be far too used to excellence to settle for mediocrity. Hrithik Roshan once memorably said: "There are great actors and then there are those who define cinema. I want to be known amongst the latter." No wonder, given his singular commitment to excellence, he's set a new benchmark for every Bollywood actor!

I think the one person who epitomises how to raise the bar is Michael Phelps, the legendary American swimmer. Immediately after winning a world-record eight gold medals at the 2008 Beijing Olympics, he started preparing himself for the London Olympics four years later! He was determined to take his swimming skills to the next level by tackling new events such as the backstroke. He said: "Right after the Olympics, our (the athletes') mindset is already focused on the next four years, and what we can do to change how we prepare and try some new things — that's something I'm looking forward to now. I've never really swum the backstroke or the 100-metre freestyle at a major international competition. So my coach is going to throw everything he has ever done coaching me out of the door and try something completely different just to see how it works. I'm excited for the next four years!" What a spirit! Most of us would be content just participating in — or just visiting — the Olympics! But look at the man who, yet in his mid-twenties, has won more Olympic gold medals than anybody else in history! He says: "I want to try something completely different." Surely he knows how to raise the bar!

RL Stine, after he'd written more than 100 books, thought he'd had enough and was about to give up writing, until he heard of a man in South America who'd presumably written 1,000 books! He decided to push himself further and wrote 150 more books thereafter! So, no matter what you've done, there is always scope to raise the bar higher. The 1-mile barrier was never run under 4 minutes until Roger Bannister broke it in 1954, and since then it has been broken hundreds of times! Likewise with the 100-metre race: Jim Hines first ran it under 10 seconds in 1968, and since then it has tumbled thousands of times! Sir Don Bradman's record of 29 Test centuries stayed unbroken for almost 40 years. But then in the last two decades, it has been broken 7 times! Every landmark is meant to be surpassed, every record meant to be broken, every accomplishment meant to be bettered. But only by those who believe in themselves, stretch themselves and raise the bar. In doing so, they redefine existing standards and yardsticks. They raise not just their own level but that of an entire populace. Their contemporaries as well as successors have new benchmarks to look up to. Next time when you envision yourself, do not think of what you do, but of what you *can* do. Always imagine yourself at your greatest glory and splendour. Firmly fixate your mind on the best you can ever be, and, by immutable laws of nature, it shall manifest. It applies to every aspect of your life. "Life is a march to perfection," Dada Vaswani once said. "Every day we must keep growing in perfection from more to more." That's our destiny, our ultimate purpose on this planet.

5

Have Your Sunny Side Up Always

Anthony D'Angelo has said this beautiful line, which is one of my favourite: "Wherever you go, no matter what the weather, always bring your own sunshine!" Having a positive disposition gives a new dimension to everything. To a sanguine person, even cloudy days seem sunny, and to a melancholic person, even sunny days seem cloudy! As they say: "It's all in the mind." Happiness or sadness doesn't exist outside, rather it dwells inside. Some people have it all, yet they are depressed, while some people are happy even if on the face of it, they don't have anything going for them.

Just like darkness can be dispelled only by light, a negative state of life can be alleviated only by a positive frame of mind. Let your mind continually dwell on positive experiences, situations, thoughts and memories. The moment any negative thought comes to mind, immediately banish it and tune in to a positive frequency. Just like we have the choice to tune in to a radio or TV channel at will, we can tune in to a desired mental broadcasting station, provided we choose to.

Like a magnet, our mind attracts what we consciously think about. The longer you dwell on a particular state, the more such circumstances will be drawn into your life. As Joel Osteen has said: "Think about what you think about." Monitor your thoughts consciously — the moment you find your thoughts teetering on the negative, catch yourself. In life, it all filters down to attitude. It has been pertinently said: "Our success is governed not by aptitude, but by attitude." Winners are who they are because of what they make of circumstances, not what the circumstances make of them. It is very easy to succumb to negative conditions. On the contrary, it takes superlative effort to stay positive. It is easy to be upbeat when everything is nice and hunky-dory around you. But only when you display optimism in the face of adversity will true, fundamental change happen in your life.

There is much profound truth in this line: "If you laugh, the whole world laughs with you, and if you cry, you cry alone." It is a little harsh, but then truth couldn't be closer. We all like to be around people who exude a happy vibe, and if somebody goes around with a sour face, we might empathise with them for a while but eventually avoid them like wildfire. Life is a journey, not a destination, and those who are positive give their fellow journeymen hope that, even if the chips are down, nothing can keep a good person out for long. Life is an interminable process of going through good times and bad, highs and lows, ebb and flow, and the sooner we accept everything in our stride and be happy nonetheless, the richer our lives are going to be.

6

Affirm Your Destiny

Alan Key once said: "The best way to predict the future is to invent it!" Of all the wonderful tools that our mind is equipped with, affirmation is the most majestic and powerful. I consider Shahrukh Khan one of the most amazing practitioners of auto-suggestion. I remember reading a magazine interview of his at the very start of his career, wherein he said: "I know I'm the very best there is!" At that time itself, I realised that it was not a cocky statement or an act of braggadocio. Rather, he was announcing emphatically to the universe that even before others accepted him as the best, he was acknowledging to himself that he was the very best. In the subsequent 18 years, I have observed that he has consistently used affirmations to further his life, career and legacy. In his commercials, movies or interviews, he always says: "Go for the best", "Dare to aspire", "Dream big", "Wish for more". That guy should know how it works: he's made it from the bylanes of Rajinder Nagar to the hearts and minds of hundreds of millions all over the world.

I personally attest to the power of affirmations. When I participated in the Grasim Mr India pageant in 2003, every day I used to vigorously proclaim in front of the mirror: "I'm coming in the Top 3." (I wish I'd said: "I'm going to win the pageant!") A strong surge of magnetic power would overwhelm me, and I would feel like I could take on anything and anybody. Whenever my faith would sag, I would start practising affirmations, and it really helped.

Some people have a tendency to dismiss affirmations as touchyfeely claptrap but let me tell you: many top athletes, artists, business people and performers all over the world generously practise self-talk. Its power and efficacy has been proven in every sphere of human activity. The age-old tradition of prayer before eating or sleeping is so that positive thoughts sink into the subconscious mind. If you look around, how many people that you've met in your life have ever used the words "I'm the best"? I can bet you'd have rarely come across anyone who does that. And the very few that do, have indeed — or are on their way to — become the very best in their field!

It must be remembered that affirmations will work only if you blend feelings with your words. You cannot be mechanical or robotic in your affirmations. Of all feelings, faith is one of the strongest. So whenever you summon your subconscious mind, do it in the spirit of faith, acceptance and belief.

The beauty about affirmations is that you can always customise them. For instance, if you're a chemist, you can say, "I'm the best chemist there is"; if you're looking for health, you can say, "I'm blessed with divine health and vigour"; if you're looking for money, you can say, "I have great wealth and abundance in my life"; if you're lonely, "My soulmate is coming into my life" or "I have a great circle of friends"; if you're angry, "I have tremendous calmness and peace"; if you want a holiday, "I'm travelling in great style and splendour!"

Don't be vague or nebulous in your self-talk. Rather, be very precise and clear. The clearer you are, the more focused your mind will be, and the swifter it will attract those conditions to itself. Also, use affirmations as frequently and as liberally as possible. Any spare time you have — taking a shower, cooking a meal, driving your car, doing household chores, etc — use it to affirm your destiny. The more frequently you use affirmations, the more powerful your life will be — that's a given.

Above all, be very careful with the words you choose. People who are perpetually talking about their problems live in abiding pain. They keep saying: "Look at me! I'm so miserable!" Any surprise why they stay stuck in a rut! As Joel Osteen has wisely said: "Don't use your words to describe your situation; rather use your words to *change* your situation." So strongly verbalise your desires and aspirations rather than your lacks and shortcomings. Put a simple experiment to work: next time you're tempted to say "What's wrong with me!" catch yourself and say "All's perfect with me!" You'll be surprised how perfect everything actually will be with you. So, use affirmations, not sporadically but consistently, and see your life change for the best.

7

Chart a New Terrain

According to a research, the very act of undertaking a new activity boosts your mental power by 15 per cent. Just imagine, if you were to undertake two new activities per year for three years — that would boost your mental capacity by almost 100 per cent! The beauty of the times we inhabit is that, regardless of inclination, skill or circumstances, there are zillions of diverse options to choose from: if you're a linguist, you could learn a new language; if you're fond of sharing your ideas with others, you could start a blog; if you're fond of socialising, you could join a dance class; if you dig sports, then tennis, swimming, golf, shooting or cricket could be up your street; if you're creative, how about undertaking a painting, sculpture, photography, sketching or pottery class; if you're an adrenaline junkie, how about river rafting? All you need to do is ask yourself what area you would like to explore or which skill you'd like to hone further, and then pursue that.

Apart from the pursuit of a hobby, even minor novelties in your day-to-day routine can do wonders to your mental fitness and alacrity. A basic thing like taking a different route than usual to your home or workplace; eating at a different restaurant or, if eating at the same one, trying a new dish; using a new shampoo, toothpaste, perfume or gel; sleeping on a different side of the bed than you usually do; calling your partner by different endearments; springing a surprise on your family by taking them for a picnic; going to a new mall for shopping; running errands that you usually don't; watching a music recital or a play instead of a movie — the possibilities are ceaseless. It is said that nothing refreshes our body and soul more than travel. How about taking a new vacation this year, instead of a usual destination? How about a cruise trip or a beach holiday instead of an outing in the hills? What's important is to keep shifting gears every now and then. It would infuse a new lease of life in you and your surroundings.

One approach that I consider ideal for myself is to make a list at the beginning of every year of new things that I want to do. For instance, here's my list for 2008:

- Write a new book
- Travel to a new destination overseas as well as in India
- Hold a photography exhibition
- Learn a new skill
- Take a cruise holiday to Alaska
- Associate with a humanitarian cause
- Do the Art of Living basic course

Out of this, I managed to accomplish some, while some I couldn't. But the underlying premise of making an annual list is that it gives me incentive to test new waters every year and to stretch my potential. Similarly, your list could be something like:

- Learn to play the piano
- Travel to Ladakh
- Learn a new language
- Indulge your parents with a holiday
- Buy a new SUV
- Gift your wife a necklace
- Learn how to swim

The options are as endless as the stars in our galaxy. From experience, I can vouchsafe that once you pursue a new activity, you will be a much more fulfilled and dynamic person than you previously were. You will then find resonance in Elanor Roosevelt's words: "The purpose of life after all is to live it, to taste the experience to the utmost, to reach out eagerly and without fear for newer and richer experiences." So go out there and chart a new terrain in order to live your life to the fullest.

8

Be a Solution Seeker

Bill Zanker once quipped: "Rich people are rich because they solve difficult problems." When Henry Ford set out to manufacture his dream car, his brief to his engineers was very simple: "I don't want to know why you can't do it. I just want to know *how* you can do it!" Eventually, his dogged spirit prevailed and, against all engineering odds in those times, the Model-automobile rolled out of the Ford factory. The best entrepreneurs or those among us that accomplish the most are not the biggest experts but the greatest solution seekers. If they don't know the answer themselves, they find the people who do. And if that's not enough, then they find the people who find the people who do. They stretch themselves and their organisations consummately to find the solution they desire.

Great breakthroughs are accomplished when the human mind is allowed to dwell on the possibilities rather than the problems. Anthony D'Angelo once said: "Focus 90 per cent of your time on solutions and only 10 per cent on problems." As the saying goes: "Even the word impossible has 'I'm possible' in it!" Considering the enormity of the human mind, and its incalculable capacity, every problem is solvable. Just by believing so, the answers will arise automatically. And once a problem has presented itself, don't procrastinate. Plunge yourself headlong into it, and gradually your higher senses will guide you to the right answer. A climber cannot get to the summit just by staring at the mountain — he or she has to start scaling it one step, one axe, one toehold at a time, and eventually get to the peak. Likewise with any problem. Break it up into a series of problems, and solve them one small step at a time. Robert H Schuller has said it best: "Success is finding a need and filling it, finding a hurt and healing it, finding a problem and solving it."

Great problems are presented to those whom great success is to eventually ensue. Setbacks come your way so that you are adequately prepared for the next level. But in order to make the progression, you have to first find solutions to existing problems. In fact, you have to shift your focus from problem to solution. Rather than thinking about how daunting a problem appears, you should think of how probable a solution seems. You will thus be undaunted by the gravity of any situation or problem. You will marshal all available resources and ordain those that are required. By focusing on the solution, you attach yourself to a rarefied frequency, one which takes only "yes" for an answer and which is capable of surmounting the greatest odds. Most people don't solve problems because they don't enlist professional help. You should associate with — rather actively seek out — those who have the expertise and the right answers. Try to solve a problem to the best of your capacity, but, if it's still beyond your reach, don't shudder to ask those in the know. Always remember: the bottom line is to solve problems, not garner popularity votes! So stretch yourself from being a problem-ponderer to a solution-seeker, and newer vistas of human capability will keep unfolding unto you. As someone has said: "Life creates the questions — we are just supposed to write the answers." So let's face up squarely to life's questions and write the answers to the best of our ability.

9

Indulge Your Mind

Most people easily understand the concept of giving nutrition to their body. They give it the best food, vitamins, minerals, and pamper it with lotions, oils, massages, unctions, and what have you. They go to great lengths to ensure that their body is well preserved and free from ailments. The slightest discomfort, and they run for medical remedies. But do they give their mind the same red-carpet treatment? On the contrary, most people treat their mind as a step sibling, or, at best, take it for granted.

Our thoughts can be likened to seeds that require nourishment to grow into fruit-bearing trees. Most people never once stop to marvel at the sheer splendour of the human mind — the awesome supercomputer inside each one of us. Comprising billions of cells, each arranged in definite patterns, the human mind is not an accident or a fluke. Neither is it there merely for the purpose of sustaining the physical body. Rather, it serves a much greater purpose — to help us progress on the path of evolution. Our mind is the veritable genie that fulfils all our wishes, obeys all our commands and makes itself so unobtrusive that it can only be felt but never seen. All that this genie ever asks of us is that it be friended with care and affection.

One of the best ways to indulge our mind is by reading. For most people, active reading stops as soon as they leave school, college or university, and for others, reading implies browsing through morning newspapers, afternoon tabloids or gossip magazines! I can't emphasise enough the importance of reading in our overall development. Our mind would be so much better if we were to undertake just 30 minutes daily of progressive reading. It could be self-help books, biographies, travelogues or on areas of your interest: cooking, gardening, martial arts, whatever. But read we must. I steadfastly keep a book on me, even when I am driving. Whenever my car stops at a red light or if I'm in a jam, instead of stressing out, I read my book and indulge my mind when all others around me are bumming out. So, in effect, I don't have to take special time out to read, and I still get to multitask and indulge my mind.

Another way that works for many is solving crossword puzzles, playing chess or sudoku. Research has proven that just like regular exercise, combined with healthy nutrition, can arrest the ageing process by 40 per cent, doing mental exercises can keep your mind healthier by up to 30 per cent.

Also, talk to people on a diverse range of topics. And, if you can, write something: again, it could be a diary, memoir, short story, random reflections, a poem, anything. It has been estimated that only 1 per cent of the human population ever bothers to write in order to reflect on their lives or express their ideas — interestingly enough, all geniuses tend to be a part of that 1 per cent who write! Since writing requires concerted focus, it brings your mental energy into play like nothing else. As Neale Donald Walsch once said: "Every time you write on paper, you write on your mind too!" So just pick up a topic close to your heart and then write on it in whatever structure or form you wish — in fact, write whatever comes into your head, even if it's complete gibberish! Give your mind the absolute freedom to flow freely and wander through an unlimited spectrum of ideas, thoughts and expressions. So read, write, talk to people, play chess, do whatever — just indulge your mind, and you will be amazed at how wonderfully it will indulge you back.

10

Ask Yourself New Questions

Jack Welch, the iconic former president of GE, wrote in his book *Winning*: "Every day in life, there is a new question. That is what keeps us going." Let's face it. We get new ideas because we ask ourselves new questions. The aircraft was invented because the Wright brothers asked themselves how humankind could fly. The telephone was invented because Alexander Graham Bell asked himself how human beings physically apart could talk to each other. The light bulb was invented because Thomas Alva Edison asked himself how darkness could be dispelled. One-day cricket was created because Kerry Packer asked how an erstwhile staid game could be revolutionised and made more entertaining and popular. The talking picture was developed by Edison because he felt that emotions could not be fully expressed in the silent talkies. The printing machine was invented because Gutenberg asked himself how literature could be circulated among the masses.

We live in times of great flux and transition. Virtually new markets and needs are being created as we read this. If we are to be of any worthwhile contribution to human evolution, we must ask ourselves new questions every now and then. We must have a dialogue with our mind like an equal, like a friend. Sometimes, when you ask yourself a new question, the mind leads you to an unfamiliar trail. Follow that trail, probe it, and a world of unceasing wonders will unfold. Human mind is the most powerful magnet. It attracts to itself all that it wants. So if you tell your mind to find a new answer for you, rest assured, it will. It might come in the form of a chance meeting with someone, a line somebody might say, or an excerpt you might read somewhere, or an idea you might get "out of nowhere," just sitting at home.

I remember when I was participating in the Grasim Mr India pageant, as part of our pre-contest preparation, we used to have a three-hour Q & A session every day, where we would be asked questions on a diverse array of topics, from politics to sports and from business to spirituality. At that time, most participants used to rile it. They were unable to see how answering 100-odd questions every day could make us better contestants! But, in hindsight, that prompted all of us to think on our feet and deepen our insights. For me, personally, that exercise was especially a blessing as it birthed my second book, *Shooting from the Lip*, a refresher manual on the question-answer round at personality pageants — perhaps I got so used to answering as well as asking questions that I found it fitting that it merited a book!

Asking new questions is an integral part of evolution, and if someone is asking you questions, feel privileged to be in a position to give answers. You never know which question might change your life! Besides, unless you ask yourself new questions, how will you find new answers? And unless you find new answers, how will you grow? In order to innovate and evolve, one has to have a sharp questioning faculty — a faculty that constantly seeks how things can be bettered and how better things can be bested. So if you want to achieve your highest potential, give yourself the gift of asking new questions, questions that stimulate the very core of your being. You'll be amazed at what the inquisitiveness will make of you.

11

Use Your Wide-angle Lens

Albert Szent-Gyorgyi, a Nobel Prize–winning biochemist, once said: "Discovery consists of looking at the same thing as every one else and thinking something different." So many times, people act like little toads, enclosed in their little wells, stoically refusing to step out of their preconditioned mindsets and lifestyles. But, all the while, God and our destiny have much bigger plans for us. We just have to look over the periphery of our wells and behold the enormous oceans that God wants us to enjoy!

I'm a photographer, and I frequently use the wide-angle lens. I know from experience that unless I open the lens to its widest angle of view, I will not be able to capture a scene to it fullest potential. Likewise, God has built in all of us a wide-angle lens. Unless we stretch it, the scene will only be marginally captured, and so much will go unharnessed. It is of supreme importance to make everything counted in life.

The higher we go in life, the more we are able to see, and vice versa. A mountaineer is able to enjoy a much more breathtaking vista at the summit than at the base camp. Likewise, a person is able to enjoy a much more expansive 360-degree view from the terrace of a building than the ground floor. The old adage "Look beyond what you see" holds tremendous veracity. Our vision should not be limited by our sights. It should be as open as the skies, as deep as the oceans. That way, even if a formidable problem presents itself, all you have to do is transfer yourself to a height of consciousness — and the problem seems minuscule.

Life is all about perspective. Again, I would correlate it photographically: if ten photographers are taking a shot from the same viewpoint, the odds are you'd get a mundane shot. However, if you stretch yourself and look for that unusual viewpoint, maybe a little farther or closer, chances are you'll get an unprecedented shot. Craig Hickman and Michael Silva give an ingenious example of perspective in their book *Creating Excellence*: "On your desk sits a 12-inch cube of ice. Now consider it from different points of view. A doctor could use it to reduce the body temperature of a fevered woman; a madman could use it to crack somebody's skull! An Eskimo wouldn't give you a dime for it; a thirsting prospector might trade you a handful of gold to get his hands on it! If you meditate on it, you soon see that even a cube of ice contains rich possibilities, limited only by your imagination!"

It's all about opening the third eye. One has to stretch one's point of view to include other — sometimes parallel and sometimes conflicting — points of view. Multiple perspectives free us to maximise our experience in life and make us grow on a holistic level.

Again, as I've repeatedly emphasised in the previous pages, most people look at things as they are, not as they *can* be. They accept the status quo docilely without bringing their imagination or capabilities into play. It is important that one looks at things objectively every now and then. Only by doing so will one get to know one's true strengths and limitations and work on them accordingly.

Swami Sukhabodhananda once beautifully said: "Most people are like an oak tree in a flowerpot. The flowerpot is like the ego and their being is like the oak tree. They should stop confining themselves to the ego. They should drop their lower self and let their higher self guide them by broadening their perspective." There is a Zen koan (quote), which says: "Before enlightenment, chopping wood, carrying water. After enlightenment, chopping wood, carrying water." Simply put, it means that regardless of circumstances, the only thing that actually changes in life is our perspective. Even if the world goes on as before, it is our approach that should get altered for a more fulfilling life. It is our perspective, above any thing else, that needs to be stretched. So let's all of us bring out our wide-angle lens, open it optimally and capture life at its fullest — we will be increasingly amazed at what all life has to offer.

Chapter Two

PHYSICALLY

"It is better to burn out than to rust away."

— Anonymous

1

Move Your Body

Our body is meant to move. Almost every creature that lives on the face of this planet is meant to move. Physical mobility is absolutely essential for sustenance, be it food gathering, reproducing, looking for shelter, protection from natural elements, and so on. In the domain of humankind, every single act of creation is carried out physically, even if it has a genesis in the mind. If you want to eat, you have to move your limbs (or if somebody else is feeding you, your mouth); while driving a car, you have to move your eyes, feet, hands, neck (and if someone is driving carelessly, your mouth!); for painting, you have to move the brush; to write, you have to move your fingers; to cook, you have to move your limbs — in virtually everything, apart from sleeping (though even in that, most people move!), your physical body comes into play.

From the tiny ant to the leviathan elephant, everything has to move to sustain itself. While in the animal kingdom, most physical movements have very rudimentary purposes — primarily a quest for survival or for procreation — in the human realm they are a lot more evolved. Since, over the centuries, we have created a very secure society built on the premise of human comfort, we no longer have to be saddled with more basic bodily pursuits like hunting for prey, looking for water, fending off ferocious beasts, etc. Consequently, most people start taking their bodies for granted. Assured that their basic necessities are met, they stop using their bodies for what they were essentially designed: to optimise the human experience.

In fact, in all of creation, we humans are the only organisms that can alter the shape and appearance of our bodies at will, and that too for purely non-biological purposes. If a horse looks the way it does, it does so unwittingly — it won't do bench presses to beef up further or go on a weight-loss regimen to look leaner! But the good thing is we humans can.

If you need any inspiration from the animal kingdom to shake you from your inertia, then mull over this fact: a tiny ant (probably one of the tiniest specimens of creation) carries 20 times its body weight on its back! And uncomplainingly at that! Reason enough for you to think twice before making fun of it again. Research after research, experiment after experiment has proven that the more we use our body, the healthier it gets. A friend of mine recently bought an offset printing machine. It has to be run for a minimum of 80 per cent of its capacity. Anything less, and it will start to malfunction. How true it is for our body as well! Unless we stretch its limits, will it not atrophy and decay? There are myriad ways to move your body: it could be hitting the gym, going for a jog in the park, doing yoga, taking the stairs instead of the lift, managing household chores, conducting your professional duties with vigour, generally committing yourself to health. The very act of moving affects the dynamics of the body and keeps it nimble. It is said that every action produces an equal and opposite reaction. Likewise, stretching yourself physically would make you stretch in every other aspect of your life and make you a consummate, well rounded person. So move your body and see your life move, like it was always destined to.

2

Free Yourself of the Biological-age Barrier

One of the maladies affecting modern society is that, regardless of which country they live in, people are stuck up on age: "So how old are you?" "You don't look 44!" "Don't tell me, she's just 18!" "He surely can't be 27!" "How can she do this at 35!" "At 67, you're too old to learn the piano!" The media also wittingly perpetrates the myth. Read any article or write-up on anybody, and, unfailingly, there is a mention of their age in that. While age is a natural phenomenon, the over-emphasis on it is humanly created. It has its roots in dread and a primal fear of decaying with time. However, research has repeatedly proven that parts of our body are literally repaired and replaced every month, others every few years. It has been scientifically proven that within seven years, every single cell in our body is replaced. That means, every seven years, we all have a brand new physical body!

However, as we read in the earlier chapter, the mind has a sacrosanct role to play in our physical existence. For centuries, people have been inundating their mind with the belief that the body is meant to decay at a certain age, that they are meant to display certain physical characteristics or look a certain way at a particular age. And, like a faithful genie, the mind obeys what you tell it and makes your self-suggestions your reality. However, by the same premise, if you were to tell yourself that age is just a number and that "my body is perpetually young" (affirmations at work again!) your mind would fulfil that wish too. Next time you feel like asking someone their age, instead of asking "How old are you?" just ask "How young are you?" That way, you will contribute to a radical shift in human consciousness vis-a-vis age.

Still, if you need to convince yourself more that age doesn't come in the way of accomplishments, spare a thought to these human age-defying dynamos:

- Alfred Eisenstaedt, one of America's legendary photographers, was commissioned by Bill Clinton and his family to take their portraits when he was 96!
- Fauja Singh ran his first marathon at the age of 89, and he is still running full marathons at the age of 98!
- Katsusuke Yanagisawa, a retired Japanese school teacher, climbed Mount Everest at the age of 71!
- Zohra Sehgal, demonstrating perpetual child-like zest, still does active theatre and film work at the age of 96!
- MF Husain, one of the greatest Indian artists of all time, still paints prolificly at the age of 94!
- Indian farmer Nanu Ram Jogi became a father at the age of 90 when he sired his 21st child!
- Minnie Munro of Australia got married at the age of 102!
- Martina Navratilova played professional tennis till the age most women become grandmothers and won a Grand Slam at the age of 50!

- Sylvester Stallone made *Rocky 6* (looking the way he looked) at 60!
- Kazumi Izaki, a mother of two, became the oldest woman in Japan to get a professional boxing licence at the age of 44!
- Wilfred Rhodes of England played a Test match against West Indies at the age of 52!
- Aruna Purohit, one of India's best-known wedding planners, started her career at the age of 50 and is still working actively at the age of 83!
- George Foreman became the oldest fighter ever to win the world heavyweight boxing crown at the age of 45!
- Khushwant Singh, one of India's most illustrious authors, is still an active writer and columnist at the age of 93!
- Judith Bharathi, a housewife and a mother from Mumbai, became a commercial airline pilot at the age of 40, while her daughter Bavicca Bharathi, ironically, completed the pilot training course in the same batch and became the country's youngest pilot at the age of 18!
- Roberta di Camerino, one of Italy's topmost fashion designers, is still active at the age of 89!
- Rabindranath Tagore took up drawing and painting at the age of 60!
- Everybody thought having a six-pack was the prerogative of teenagers, but Shahrukh Khan and Aamir Khan got theirs after the age of 40!
- George Bernard Shaw wrote a play at the age of 94!
- Diana Athill won the prestigious literary prize Costa Book Award at the age of 91!

- Jessica Tandy won the Best Actress Oscar at the age of 80!
- Éamon de Valera, was elected president of Ireland at the age of 84!
- Hiroshi Hoketsu of Japan competed in the Beijing Olympics at the age of 67, returning to the Olympics after 44 years!
- George Brunstad of the US swam across the English Channel at the age of 70!
- Kimani Nganga of Kenya became the world's oldest person to start school at the age of 84!

What do you think is common among all these people? They kept stretching themselves and refused to accept the biological-age barrier. They kept pushing, what other people thought were, the limits governed by time and age. Fauja Singh, the world's oldest marathon-runner at 98, once said: "I run because I hope to inspire young people to keep going and older people never to give up." But the best insight I got on the age phenomenon was from the legendary MF Husain, while interviewing him for this book. When I asked him what message he'd like to give the youth, he said matter-of-factly: "What message can I give them — I still feel like I'm one among the youth myself!" If he, at 94, feels that way then I'm sure almost everyone who's reading this book will take heart and be impelled to say: "Wow! I'm still young to do whatever I want to do!" As the saying goes: "Age is what you make of it." So go ahead and make the very best of your biological age — no matter what others say, it is all in the mind!

3

Create Exercise Time

We live in pressure-prone times governed by deadlines and mandates, where everything has to be done yesterday! But still there is absolutely no excuse for neglecting oneself. Most people give the alibi that they're too busy to exercise. I think Barack Obama, the current US president, is one of the busiest people on the face of this planet. Nonetheless, no matter where he is, he works out for one hour every day, doing weight-training, running on the treadmill and shooting basketball hoops. Asked how he finds the time, this is what he says: "Most of my workouts have to come before my day starts. There's always a trade-off between sleep and working out!" Likewise for his predecessors: George W Bush was an avid mountain biker, Bill Clinton jogged around Washington and George HW Bush liked to golf, jog and play tennis. If, despite their compelling schedules, all these American presidents could maintain such exemplary exercise routines, then most of us can manage to spare at least 20 minutes out of our daily schedules, no matter how "daunting" they might be! It has been documented by American researchers that over 80 per cent CEOs and presidents of blue-chip companies apportion time for a physical activity, be it golf, tennis, swimming, squash, etc, at least thrice a week. No wonder, their devotion to fitness reflects in their financial bottomlines as well!

Anil Ambani, one of the wealthiest men in the world, is a classic example of the will surmounting the schedule! He was once 105 kilos and couldn't walk one kilometre in an hour. Today, he tips the scale at 68 kilos and runs the Mumbai marathon every year! How does he do it? He gets up at 4 in the morning and goes for a run on Mumbai's streets for almost 10–15 kilometres every day. He knows that through the day, he'd get stuck in the rigmarole of board meetings and other details that accompany managing one of the world's biggest corporate empires, so he creates exercise time early in the morning and sticks to it, come what may.

Today, most people are plagued with ailments because of inertia and idleness, rather than over-activity. I think we live in times where it's simply great to have the conveniences and easy amenities of modern life. It's such a wonderful gift of science that we have dishwashers, microwaves, washing machines, vacuum cleaners, etc, freeing up a tremendous amount of our time which we can employ judiciously. However, most of us fritter away that time in vacuous gossip, idleness, trivial banter or TV time. Leisure time can be used very constructively for exercise, provided you're willing. Regardless of what you do, you can apportion your daily schedule such that no matter what, you take some time out for exercise on a regular basis. When you consider the benefits that accrue from regular exercise — youthful appearance, stronger body, better health, more endurance, greater immunity — it's an investment worthiest of consideration. Come to think of it, what are fifteen minutes or half an hour daily if you consider a lifetime of health and fitness? Most people consider bonds, stocks and shares as investment, when in fact the real investment is in you and your body, the only asset that is effectively yours! Let your work never be a subterfuge for exercise laxity. If you're keeping long hours at your workplace, you can consider keeping an exercise bike or a treadmill there, or, if that's not possible, how about walking fours lengths of your office or climbing up and down a flight of stairs. Alternatively, if you are an early morning person, you could go for a walk or jog before getting into the rigours of your work. And if you work out of a home office, then what could be better? You have the luxury of time and the benefit of a self-orchestrated routine. All you have to do is to take the initiative to exercise. And in order to create a schedule that you'd adhere to in the long-term, apportion your time in such a way that it respects the uniqueness of your lifestyle — no point getting up early in the morning and going for a jog if let's say you sleep only at 2 in the night! Just listen to the rhythm of your life, create some quality exercise time and your body will align itself beautifully. As with every other concept in this book, all that it takes is willingness and commitment. And once you decide that you are going to create worthwhile exercise time, come what may, then the fog of excuses and alibis will dissipate, and you will magically have all the time you desire at your disposal!

4

Make Your Appearance Count

Most people, regardless of how substantive or shallow they are, tend to notice others by their appearance. It is a pure law of aesthetics. My yoga teacher, Yogi Ashok, a great spiritual man himself, once recounted me this story: One day, Mahatma Gandhi went to meet Rabindranath Tagore. Gandhiji, himself a very austere man, was getting restless waiting for Tagore while the latter went through his elaborate grooming rituals. Tagore was a man of aesthetics, given to the concept of human beauty. When he finally emerged from his chamber, Gandhiji asked him why he placed so much emphasis on appearance. He replied: "I take care to dress up because, one, I like it, and, two, I feel it offends the other person's sensibilities if I have an unkempt appearance. I think I do a tremendous service to others by giving them a model of visual refinement. That way I create a much more appealing world." An amazing theory, don't you think!

Imagine what a garden would be like if it has all the elements — grass, trees, flowers, hedges — but only in name.

What if the grass is full of weed, the trees are asymmetrical, the flowers are withered and the hedges are unmanicured! Would you like to visit that garden? Won't you feel offended by its slovenliness? On the contrary, what attracts you most to a botanical garden? Lush grass, verdant trees, manicured flowerbeds and sylvan hedges. Likewise with the human form. Much as we would like to believe otherwise, someone with an uncouth appearance puts us off, regardless of how much substance is latent in them. On the contrary, someone really fetching instantly uplifts our senses. Even the most exalted seers and yogis wear spotless robes and have a special beauty about them. There is a reason we naturally get drawn to attractive people. Keep aside the fact that after a while some of them put us off due to their vanity and preoccupation with themselves. But what is our natural, primal reaction? That of attraction.

From time immemorial, human beings have beautified themselves to attract the opposite gender. Sexist as it sounds, it has been one of the most rudimentary aspects of the mating game. After centuries of evolution, we are no different. In fact, with the sheer smorgasbord of beauty devices at our disposal, it is actually a waste not to devote more time to your appearance. It's not like you have to frequent parlours, salons or spas all the time to look your best. Following a healthy diet, exercising regularly, taking adequate rest and placing emphasis on personal hygiene goes a long way in ensuring that you are at your immaculate best always. But, yes, if you feel like, a monthly visit to the salon for a pedicure, facial and the works should be had by all means. Life is a process of refinement, and if you find something assists you in that at any stage, why not? For as someone once said: "The greatest gift that you can give yourself is a little bit of your own attention!" If the outside is a reflection of the inside, and after you've devoted attention to cleaning the inside, then is it not logical that the outside should be clean as well? Next time you're tempted to equate slovenliness with spirituality, just think of some of the most spiritual figures you've known of in history. When you see how divine their appearance was, you will automatically get the hint!

5

Worship Your Body

Our body is the most supreme gift we can ever have on the material plane. When we were born, our body was the only asset we ever had (before the nurse or midwife clothed us), and when we pass on, our body is the last asset we will ever relinquish. It is the only thing that will always be with us till we are alive, 24 hours a day, 7 days a week, throughout our lives. No matter how expensive a dress you buy or how ornate a piece of jewellery you don, you still take them off before sleeping, wear them sparingly and probably discard them after a few years. Likewise, no matter how close a loved one is to you, you cannot keep them with you twenty-four-by-seven. They will have their own existence to lead too. But our body remains with us faithfully, even if everything else deserts. So, in effect, our body is the foremost thing worthy of worship on the material, earthly plane.

Our body is a veritable shrine, and the more we worship it, the better our lives will be. It has been said that self-love is one of the highest forms of love. That also includes loving your body. Because apart from sleeping — though even in that, there is a body-awareness at some level — I can't think of a single activity where your body does not come into play. So worship it, and it will give you the most wonderful instrument to work with. Just like the more we deposit in our bank accounts, the higher our security buffer, the more we invest in our health and worship our body, the better our quality of life will be. Treat your body like your best friend, and next time you feel like overlooking it, just remember how it would feel like overlooking your best friend!

You can't even begin to imagine how priceless the human body is! Consider this example: If somebody were to give you Rs 50 crore and ask for one of your fingers in return, would you part with it? Chances are (if one is not insane or desperate), you would never do it. So if one finger of yours is worth that much (at least), then your body, with all its organs, would be worth hundreds of thousands of crores! When people are calculating somebody's wealth, they just take into account their paper money or notional wealth. While in reality, you already are worth hundreds of thousands of crores (at least)! So if at all you are to pride yourself on any asset, let that be your body. Worship it and see it appreciate incalculably in value.

Most people, since they have such limited awareness, look condescendingly on those who indulge their body and give it the attention it richly deserves. Please overlook such people and their trivial reactions. Your body is yours alone to preserve and nurture. Should it malfunction, none of the snide-remarkers are going to come and save it. So ignore all else and singularly worship your body. At the same time, however, remember there is a fine line between indulgence and vanity. Worship your body but don't be a narcissist, take care of it but don't be a fetishist. Give equal attention to your mind and soul as you would to your body, but definitely not any less. Only if there is a balance and equilibrium between all three will you actually flourish in life and be truly fulfilled.

6

Harmonise Your Breath

An ancient Tibetan spiritual master once said: "Breath *is* life." If we observe subliminally, our breath is the thing closest to us, nearest to us. To be able to breathe a smooth, harmonious breath is a great blessing. It revitalises and cleanses you, infusing your mind with a vigour and a certainty of purpose. The greatest service you can actually do to your health is to make your breath naturally harmonious.

Most people go through life totally oblivious to their breath. They pay no heed whatsoever to it. In doing so, they ignore the greatest essence, the greatest power at humankind's disposal. Linesh Sheth once wrote in *The Speaking Tree*: "The simplest way to build a harmonious relationship with life is to develop a loving, joyful relationship with your breath. As you breathe, so shall you live!" Just the very simple, conscious act of breathing slowly and deeply five minutes, twice a day, with a smile and closed eyes, will give you a feeling of joy in all those organs where you perceive the silken touch of breath. The purpose is to stretch yourself by prolonging and deepening your breath.

Medical science has proven that longevity is directly related to respiratory rate. A simple comparison substantiates this: a mouse breathes 150 times a minute and lives for 1 year; a dog breathes 22 times a minute and lives up to 10 years; a human being breathes 12 times a minute and has an average life expectancy of 75 years; a turtle breathes 3 times a minute and can live up to the grand age of 200 years!

You should look at your breath as if it were your constant and unfailing friend. Most people breathe shallow. They are unmindful of the essence of life latent in the very act of breathing. As Guru Nanak once said: "A human being is a creature of breath, one breath at a time. If breath comes, we are humans, otherwise but a mound of clay!" Actually, if you realise, there is always only one breath separating life and death. That's how sacred — and sacrosanct — breath is!

Deep breathing brings about a very calming, tranquil sensation. As Linesh has beautifully said: "When you pay attention to the beauty with which life rests within you, for the first time, you will experience what it is to feel alive." Just by watching your breath, you will begin to experience a deep sense of peace. If you breathe with great satisfaction, you will feel the grace of life. How frequently you breathe, and the regularity with which you do it, will impact the proportion of well-being you will feel. Always remember, breath is all. As Guru Ding Le Mei wrote in his book *My Life in Tibet*: "To live in tune with the universe, we must live in harmony with its laws. The basis of universal law is the rhythm of the great and holy breath of life. Truly, breath is the master key to all the laws." So breathe harmoniously, and harmony will become the emblem of your life.

Chapter Three

SPIRITUALLY

"The noblest journey that anyone can undertake is the evolution of their spirit."

— Anonymous

1

Have an Unshakeable Faith

Faith, they say, can move mountains. I have personally experienced the power of faith very palpably. When I entered the Grasim Mr India pageant, nobody (apart from Ronicka, my parents and my sister) thought that I had a chance. But I felt a strong power within me surging me on. I felt that God was working through me, and no matter how capable or prepared the others were, I would outshine. I remembered what they say about the bumblebee: "The laws of aerodynamics state that the bumblebee can't fly. But somebody forgot to tell that to the bumblebee — unaware, it keeps flying!" So if a tiny bumblebee can challenge the very laws of physics unaware, imagine what a full-grown, fully aware human being can do, backed by the power of faith! As the *Bible* says: "According to your faith, so be it done to you." Even when a situation looks bleak, you must march forward by the power of faith. A philosopher has beautifully said: "O Soul, why do you worry? What if difficulties come! Along with every difficulty also comes the remover of the difficulty. Let your gaze be fixed on the remover and not on the difficulty." Should adversity ever come, all you have to do is to remember God with deep love, sincerity and faith, and it will work as your magic wand.

Margaret Shepherd has said this beautiful line: "Sometimes the only transportation required is a leap of faith!" When all else seems illogical or lost, that's when human faith steps in to work miracles. Faith can create, bind, amend and harmonise. If given carte blanche and a free hand, faith can arrange you a meeting with Barack Obama (or Madonna, if you so desire!) or make you top the IAS exam. All you need to do is stretch it and let it run with freedom and abandon. Tell your faith that you can work magic in tandem with it and manifest all that you desire.

At most intersections in life, faith is the only salve. It is by faith alone that leaders are able to motivate their followers, and captains are able to spur their team members. Every single religion originates from faith, many people do business purely on faith. True faith must be indomitable. Reason and rationale are not the touchstones of faith, nor the requisites one should measure it by. Just like you don't really need to know how electrical current works to enjoy electricity, or how a car's engine works to enjoy a car ride, you don't really need to know how faith works. In that sense, faith is like a medicine. When a doctor tells you that a medicine will work for you, you don't really need to know every ingredient or constituent chemical in order to benefit from it. The very fact that a doctor tells you that a medicine will work is sufficient. Likewise with faith. If you try to analyse too much, you are doing yourself a disservice. JUST HAVE FAITH IN FAITH — read that sentence repeatedly till it gets driven into your subconscious. Its miraculous powers are way too great to be put to scrutiny. Just like you don't really need to see earth rotating on its axis to know that it does, ditto with faith. It is an immutable fact. Suffice to know that faith works, not how it does. As Napoleon put it: "All scholastic scaffolding falls as a ruined edifice before that one single word: Faith!" And as Emerson said: "Faith makes us and not we it; and faith makes its own forms!" So stretch your faith — and watch it make its own awe-inspiring forms for you!

2

Life is Beautiful, No Matter What

Someone once said: "The best gifts in life come in soiled packages." One has to just uncover the outer packing to discover the uniqueness of the gift. It might hurt momentarily but when you look in retrospect, you realise even a setback or a disappointment happened for the best.

There was a time in my life, when I was trying to make it big as an actor. For almost one and a half years, I tried my best, but nothing worked out. Audition after audition yielded the same disappointment. It was during this duration that, encouraged by Ronicka, I developed an interest in photography, and gradually it became my profession. Today, by God's supreme grace, I do rewarding assignments all over the world and can gratefully say this: I am infinitely happier and more fulfilled than I'd have otherwise been. So, as it turned out, my failure as an actor prompted me into a far greater success as a photographer. God's amazing plan, isn't it!

So many times you realise the benefit of something after it has passed. Once, my wife and I were boarding a flight from

Bahrain to Delhi. We had already rescheduled our ticket once earlier, and when we reached the airport we discovered that the flight was full. We tried to plead, but the person at the check-in counter expressed her helplessness. But, providentially, after giving us a patient hearing, she offered us two seats on first-class in the subsequent flight six hours later. Did we complain? You bet not! Many a time, we've had a shoot cancelled or deferred — only to have it replaced by a much bigger and more promising account later on, or with something unrelated to work but deeply satisfying on a personal level. It has happened to us with such regularity that we now know that whenever such a thing happens, it is for the best.

My all-time favourite credo is: "Life is beautiful, no matter what." I have made it my abiding dictum in life to believe that *all* that happens, happens for the best. I strongly suggest you do the same. Don't be one of those who keep waiting for something "big" to happen to enjoy the beautiful joyride that life is. Savour each and every nuance and occurrence in life. Just like an ocean is made up of infinitesimal drops, a journey is made up of small steps, the universe is made up of minuscule atoms and a mountain is made up of little rocks, our life is made up of tiny moments, each one of which serves its purpose in our evolution. Always look at your life as a continuum, rather than a disjointed series of fragmented moments. The moment you resolve to enjoy your life, right then and there, every moment becomes propitiously enjoyable. There is untold bliss in the simple pleasures of life: saying "I love you" to somebody, a child's smile, a delicious meal, sound sleep, cool breeze, beautiful sky, an entertaining movie, soothing music, flowers in bloom, a refreshing shower, and so on. Start finding your happiness not in what will be, but in what *is*. Even if you're sitting in an enclosed room with nothing to do, you can at least appreciate the fact that you're in the midst of tranquillity, away from chaos and noise!

No matter where you are, you can always find something beautiful to appreciate. Nobody has demonstrated it better than Viktor Frankl, a Jewish survivor of the German concentration camps during World War II. In his book, *Man's Search for Meaning*, he describes a bowl of filthy water with a fish head floating in it, given to him by his Nazi captors. He conditioned his mind to see the beauty in this meal rather than focus on the horror of it! He conceded that it was his ability to see the beauty in everything that helped him survive those inhuman camps. Imagine, if Viktor could see beauty even in those extremely savage circumstances, most of us are infinitely more fortunate! All we have to do is to look around — and within — and select beauty as our focus. Rest assured, we'll invariably find something beautiful to experience — something which we might have till now taken for granted!

3

Have a Frequent Communion with God

Swami Vivekananda once said: "With God you can sail over the high seas. Without God, you cannot cross a threshold." I can strongly say that the greatest blessing in my life is that I can have a communion with God on anything and everything I want. This healthy relationship has ensured that I am totally secure in whatever I do in life, for as someone has said: "The only worthwhile security that one can ever have is the one that comes from within." That internal dialogue with God is of utmost importance. It should be our earnest endeavour to make it not a one-off exchange or a sporadic remembrance, as is the case with most people in times of distress. Why not stretch your dialogue to include even times of joy? And, gradually, why not come to a level whereby you need the refuge of neither sadness nor happiness to commune with God? Whereby you engage in a communion just for communion's sake. The best part is, you don't have to go anywhere to have this exchange.

As Franz Kafka, the Austrian philosopher, has so beautifully said: "You need not leave your room. Remain sitting at your table and listen. You need not even listen, simply wait. You need not even wait, just learn to become quiet and still and solitary. The world will freely offer itself to you to be unmasked. It has no choice; it will roll in ecstasy at your feet." When you actually demonstrate that calmness, the dialogue with God becomes very natural and free and spontaneous.

Suppose, if children deeply want something, who should they logically go to? Their parents, right! Likewise, if we deeply want something, who should we approach? Our eternal parent, God, right! Work on this sacrosanct relationship, and make it the cornerstone of your life. Once Mother Teresa was asked what message she would like to give humanity. She replied: "People should pray more." Your relationship with God should be that of a best friend, that of a child with a parent. (You can worship God in the mother or father form, however you feel. Though I've referred to God as him throughout this book, yet there is no binding on you. Feel free to refer to him as her or it, however you wish.) Let there be no long-winded dogma of a formal equation between you and God. Once you make God your sole point-of-reference, everything else becomes simpler and clearer.

Above everything, God should be real to you. You must walk with him. You must talk with him. He should be your closest partner, your ally. Very often people get stuck in a pre-determined approach to God, supplicating him with archaic hymns, chants and prayers, emphasising the words much more than the feelings. The most effective way to communicate with God is how you would communicate with yourself: simple, uncluttered, unobtrusive and in the first person. Moreover, form your relationship with God not out of fear but out of love. Don't say, as most people do, "I'm God-fearing"; say "I'm God-loving". And don't make this communion a ritual or a chore, like praying at pre-designated times or on fixed occasions through the day. Don't confine your remembrance to a Sunday, Monday or Friday, and forget it the rest of the week! Remember God as much as you can and as many times as you can. God is the foundation, the bulwark on which the very existence of our lives is based. The stronger this bulwark is, the happier and more complete our lives will be. I repeat: don't remember God only at special times — if you remember him (or her) at all times, then all times are going to be special, *very* special indeed. As Sri Sri Ravi Shankar has said: "God is the substratum of this universe, the basis of this existence. God is the space in which all things happen." The blessedness of communion brings you to a state where God ceases to be an object or a subject, but becomes an experience! Just like a tree should always remember its roots (otherwise it'd be lifeless) and a river should know its source (else it will have no life), we should always know and be connected with our ultimate source: God.

4

Make God Unlimited

Like many other departments of their life, most people also limit their miracle producer: God. They relegate themselves to a life of mediocrity, thinking that this is the life God ordained them to live, that this is God's will for their life. But as this line from *Conversations with God* puts it: "Your will for you is God's will for you!" In other words, if people want to be mediocre and lead substantial lives, what can God do for them? We'd used the parent-child analogy in the previous sub-chapter vis-à-vis God and a human being. Imagine, if a child does not want to study, the parents can't force them to! They can only help them to a certain point, but after a while, the child will be left to their own devices. No matter how much effort a mother puts in, she cannot physically take the examinations for her child. Likewise, God helps us all.

Making God unlimited is making yourself unlimited and vice versa. Tell yourself that if you follow your heart, and all the other laws of nature, God can (and will) virtually do anything for you. But you will have to strongly *believe* in his power. Stretch the scope of what God can do for you. His ways are much greater and vaster than even the limits of your non-limits can reach. So when you have such an incalculable power at your behest, optimise it. Take it to the next level. Say to yourself: "God, you can do through me what everyone else considers undoable; you can get me what everyone else thinks is ungettable; you can make that possible for me what everyone else deems impossible!" When you have this dialogue, see how God takes a front seat and gives you a joyride into the wonderland of abundance. Borrowing again from the parent-child analogy: If a child is going through any kind of duress, who should they logically approach? Their parents, right! And, on top of it, if the child knows that their parents are very wealthy, then all the more reason to feel financially secure. Would it not be foolishness if the child goes about supplicating and begging others for handouts when the parents are overflowing with abundance? Likewise with us and God, our parent. He who is omnipotent, all-abundant, is waiting for us to share in his bounty. But it is his children who have gone adrift and are seeking morsels from other, much lesser sources. They go from pillar to post, beseeching others, blaming others, soliciting others, riling others, thinking they have done enough. But they haven't done what they should actually do: ask their parent rightfully! In order to make their life abundant, all they need to do is to call on the Holy Father (or Mother) and his (or her) limitless abundance. In the wake of their magic, all limitations will cease to be, and we will be as abundant as the power that has so lovingly created us.

5

Stretch Your Tolerance Threshold

One of the most denigrating human characteristics is the notion of superiority, of being better than others. People from all cultures, tribes, ethnicities and religions are vehemently convinced of their superiority over others. Not just that, we see ample cases of even countries demonstrating this superiority-driven intolerance over other countries. Most of the bloodshed and violence in today's world is perpetratred by this Frankenstein called intolerance whom people have cultivated over countless centuries and nurtured through their thoughts, myths and fables. Most of what is undesirable today stems from people's attachment to their religion. They have become so fanatic and dogged in their mistaken superiority that the concept of "one world, one people" is alien to them. They never stretch their tolerance threshold beyond their own clans and cliques. They become like a fetid garden with only one kind of smell, only one colour. Imagine what a rainbow would be like if it comprised of only violet! Or what would that garden be like if it had only one kind of flower! Or, if it had only grass and nothing else! Can you recollect spending time with a rigid and orthodox person? Do you recall what it felt like afterwards? You must have felt so negative that you wanted to purge your entire being. At the same time, can you recall being with someone who is liberal, open and permissive? Do you recall how positive and elevated you felt afterwards?

It becomes our supreme duty to make this a much better and more holistic world for our coming generations. Imagine, what kind of parents would give their children toxic food? The most unthinkably appalling! Almost every parent would want to give their child the healthiest nutrition. Likewise, should they also not give them the ambrosia of permissiveness, love and open-heartedness? Let our hearts be open, not just our minds. Let's stretch ourselves to believe that the entire world is our family, not just a select few. One can make a worthy contribution to civilisation not by consuming the potion of hatred but only by consuming the nectar of tolerance.

Let's consider an analogy: if you were to go to the US, you can go via UK, Italy, Germany, France, the Gulf or take a straight transatlantic flight. None of them are the right or the wrong way. It all depends on your preference, choice of airline, budget or travel plans. Similarly, if you go to a restaurant, you can order anything from the wide variety of dishes on the menu or request something off the menu. There is no right or wrong dish. So just like taking a travel sector or ordering a dish is strictly a matter of personal taste and preference, there are multiple ways to reach God. Just like a parent would feel hurt if you were to compare their children or say that one child is good and the other bad, God would be very hurt if you were to say that one way to approach him is good and the other bad. Always remember that all ways lead to God eventually and are equally worthy of respect and admiration.

6

Give Yourself the Gift of Gratitude

In all that I have seen of life, I have discovered that the greatest gift is the gift of gratitude. It is the best blessing that anyone can be endowed with. I can say from personal experience that you must express gratitude regardless of your present station in life. Even when I was going through a turbulent phase, I had only words of gratitude for my circumstances, for I knew that one day "this too shall pass". Actually, if you develop a thankful attitude in life, things around you start being more harmoniously aligned and in accordance with your plans.

I always used to read how we should be thankful for something even before we receive it. I did not know how true it was until I practised it. I always loved travelling, and there was a phase in my mid-twenties when I just couldn't travel for several years. When I read about the "thanking in advance" practice in *The Power of Positive Thinking,* I started to thank God beforehand for making me travel to the most exotic destinations in the best style possible. After a while, my gratitude became intense, and I started to feel that I have already come back from the place that I wanted to actually visit. Within a year I started travelling again, just the way I wanted to. It's been four years, and I have travelled to the farthest parts of the world from Auckland to Alaska, all thanks to — you guessed it! — the spirit of thankfulness. I simply recommend that you do the same and manifest whatever you want in life. The more thankful you are, the more reasons you shall have to be thankful for. Actually, if your vocabulary were limited to just one word — thanks — you will cakewalk through life than if it were laced with the most bombastic and hifalutin words, devoid of emotion and feeling.

And don't limit your gratitude to only the special gestures and occasions. Rather, make it a consistent habit to thank for everything and everyone in your life — to thank for the very act of life itself. Look at yourself, and you will see a multitude of things to be grateful for: your very breath, eyesight, voice, arms, legs, ears, hair, and so on. Look further away, and the list will be equally exhaustive: your family, friends, peers, people you look up to, and so on. And then there is the ever-enchanting nature — greenery, landscape, birds, flowers, etc — that one can be thankful for.

Gratitude is the antidote to most of life's sufferings. In fact, all of us would benefit enormously from a simple exercise: count-your-blessings exercise! Take a paper and a pen, and list 30 things for which you are grateful to God. You could write whatever you genuinely feel. It could be anything, from your family to eyesight to career to a full head of hair or a sports car standing in the porch! It'd help enormously if you could look at, around or within you, close your eyes once and enumerate all that you are grateful for. Do this as often as possible, but especially when you feel low. You'd instantly feel cheerful and upbeat.

Exercise your gratitude generously. And don't make it dependant on an occasion or event, as many people assume. Every moment you should thank God for all that has been, is or will be. The higher your gratitude, the better your life will be. Denis Waitley has said it best: "Happiness cannot be travelled to, owned, earned, worn or consumed — it is the spiritual experience of living every minute with love, grace and gratitude." So let's be grateful, and happiness will naturally follow.

Chapter Four

FINANCIALLY

"It is not only my right and my privilege to walk in the abundance God has for me — it is my responsibility."

— Jan Denise

1

Dream Abundance

It has been aptly said: "Life is a just employer — it gives you what you ask for!" All you have to do is to stake your claim in the ever-abundant cosmic pie. There is enough in the universe for everyone. As Rhonda Byrne says in *The Secret*: "Whatever you ordain, by the law of attraction, you will have that!"

Don't be embarrassed to desire abundance. It's not as if those who live in poverty are doing this world any greater service than those who live in affluence. Poverty is a state of mind that fulfils itself as readily as abundance. One should continually aspire towards God's largesse and his bounty, which is unlimited. If there were only limited wealth in the universe, then going by simple mathematics, with the colossal number of people added every year, everybody's income and wealth would have decreased! But we all know that's not true. In fact, the universe itself has been expanding for the past 13.7 billion years, and till date it is! Likewise with the wealth and riches in the world — the more the people, the greater the pie grows. This is an absolute law. Just like nature giving all of itself freely: if it rains in a city, it rains equally for everyone; if it's sunny, it's equally sunny for everyone. Likewise, the universe offers its bounties to everyone, regardless of nationality, age, status, colour, creed or religion. All it wants is you to *want* it! Most people have a scrimping-and-scrawling mentality where they just want to get by. They feel they want *just* this much. They keep limiting their desires and dreams. But the universe wants you to dream unlimited. It wants you to be so profuse in your aspirations that even "abundant" would not be a sufficient word!

It's been wisely said: "As you sow, so shall you reap." If you sow dreams of abundance, you will manifest abundance in your life. If you convince yourself on an intrinsic level that you can have all that you want, then you will eventually have all that you want. It's very important that you inundate yourself with thoughts of prosperity, affluence and wealth. Speak consciously of abundance and use words that demonstrate your wealth-consciousness. Even if thoughts of deprivation come to you, quickly brush them aside. If others around you are pettifogging or talking of lack, circumvent the small talk. Associate yourself with surplus — and surplus shall become your cornerstone. Actually, every self-made person has come upon wealth by first visualising themselves wealthy, and subsequently the universe has merely responded. So dream abundance, and eventually it will become your reality. As Dr Wayne Dyer has said: "Abundance is not something we acquire — it is something we tune into!"

The universe wants us to have better than the best. Napoleon Hill once said: "Money cannot move, think or talk, but it can 'hear' when a man who desires it, calls it to come!" So call money emphatically, and it will come to you in heaps.

2

Live a First-class Lifestyle

Most people aspire to lead a king's life. But there is one thing that deters them from doing so — deep down they are convinced that that life is *not* for them! That they can't afford it. My experience suggests that people who lead an affluent life are determined to do so, no matter what. Long ago, I read one of Amitabh Bachchan's interviews. He spoke of an instance in early 2000 when he was in deep red financially and on the verge of bankruptcy. He was on an international flight, and, after dinner, the airhostess came with the merchandise trolley. A connoisseur of watches, he really liked a Swiss timepiece. It was prohibitively expensive. He thought for a second and said: "If at all I have to go down, I might as well go down in style!" He went ahead and bought the watch with all the money he had on him. To anyone else, it might sound like financial harakiri. But, as luck would have it, a few weeks later he signed the KBC contract. His future made an about-turn, and he has never looked back since!

I will again share a first-hand experience with you: A friend of mine nurtured the dream of travelling business-class by air for a long time. The first time she travelled to the US five years ago, though she was financially not doing so well, she booked herself a business-class ticket, taking the tab on her credit card. It did pinch her, but she said, "What the heck!" and went ahead nonetheless. She came back, and her work prospered so much that it's been five years, she's taken 18 international trips — and every single time she's flown business-class! Awesome, isn't it? The moral of the story is: if you *really* want to live a first-class lifestyle (and there's no reason why every human being should not!), then all you have to do is to convince yourself on a deep, fundamental level that that's how God intended you to do it — live life king-size or queen-size — and rightfully claim it as yours.

As Joel Osteen says in *Your Best Life Now*: "You must keep in mind that you are a child of the Most High God and were created for great things. God didn't make you to be average. God created you to excel, and He's given you ability, insight, talent, wisdom and His supernatural power to do so. You have everything you need right now to fulfil your God-given destiny." He further says: "Just like one's children's poverty is a direct reflection on that person as a parent, similarly when one goes through life with a poverty mentality, it is not glorifying to God. God is not pleased when one drags through life, defeated, depressed, perpetually discouraged by circumstances. Rather, God is pleased only when one develops a prosperous mindset." So proclaim your rightful position as a child of God and know that everything is within your reach. See yourself in affluence, see yourself soaring to higher levels. And keep that vision enshrined in you with constancy.

While living an abundant life, please don't be saddled with guilt. Ask yourself, do you want to give contaminated food to yourself or your family? You don't, right! You want to have the best quality, and rightfully so. Likewise, why not apply the same to the other areas of your life! If you're going to wear clothes anyway (unless nudism is the preferred way for you!), then why not wear the very best? Likewise, if you're driving a car, then why drive a beat-up ramshackle (which also harms the environment by releasing more toxins)? Why not drive the latest with the best safety and emission norms? Why not fill up your car with extra-premium fuel instead of regular? Why not go for the best furnishings and fixtures for your house? Why not go for the very best*est* in everything? Seriously, it's not a question of affordability — it's just a question of choice.

3

Take Risks

Sabeer Bhatia once said: "The greatest risk in life is not to take a risk." I have learnt this from personal experience: the bigger the risk, the bigger the gain. In 2006, I'd promised my wife Ronicka that we'd publish her maiden coffee-table book, *The Eye of Eternity*, and have it launched by style icon Malaika Arora Khan. It was a significant project at that time that demanded an investment of about Rs 15 lakh. We had just got married, and that was all the saving we had at that time. Yet, we decided to go ahead with the project, investing all our money, convinced deep down that the gamble would pay off. And we were right. Within a year, that investment paid itself over several times. Had we been unwilling to take the risk and stretch ourselves, that project and the subsequent success might have never seen the light of day. You've got to alter the mindset. Relinquish the cocoon of comfort and acquire the spirit of challenge. As the saying goes: "You cannot soar with the eagles as long as you're pecking around with the chickens!" In other words, you cannot reap big dividends unless you take big risks. You cannot live a grand life unless you stake high.

In the book *Think Big & Kick Ass*, Bill Zanker narrates an awesome example of risk-taking. He tells us how he was a small-time event promoter till one day he had a brainwave. He thought it'd be amazing to have Donald Trump as the key speaker in his motivation school. Spurred by the idea, he offered Trump $10,000 to speak to his students, which was a first for Zanker, as before that his speakers had come gratis. Trump flatly refused. A week later, Zanker upped the offer to $25,000. But still to no avail. The subsequent week, Zanker raised it to $100,000. Still he was given a cold shoulder. Then he sat down with himself and thought how much he wanted to get Trump to speak. After a lot of rumination, he realised that he was *desperate* to get Trump — probably there was nothing more that he wanted in his entire life! That moment was an epiphany for Zanker. He immediately picked up the phone, held his breath and offered Trump $1 million — 100 times more than his initial offer! Trump took one hour to deliberate and called back. He agreed on the condition that he'd speak to an audience of at least 10,000. Zanker agreed and closed the deal. When he hung up the phone, he went to the toilet — and threw up! Because, one, till then he was just about making that much money as profit in an entire year, and, two, the maximum attendance that Zanker had managed till then in his 25-year-long career was only 700! But he composed himself. He had taken a stratospheric risk and was very determined to make it work. He created an aggressive marketing plan and billed the event as a Wealth Expo with Donald Trump as the key speaker. His promotion strategy was to encourage people to meet Trump, one of the most successful people in the world, and learn first-hand his secrets of wealth-creation. Commensurate with the risk he had taken, eventually not 10,000 but 31,500 people attended the event! As a result, it eventually was very easy to pay Donald Trump his fee! Zanker later said: "That experience proved to me beyond any doubt that when you think big, big things come to you. I had bet big, and I won." So take risks — even if at times it means forking out 100 times more than you've initially imagined! — and live the life of your dream. It always pays back!

The universe, in fact, by its very nature, doesn't let any of its creations fall. If you observe carefully, it's an absolute marvel: Even when the earth is upside down, it doesn't let anybody or anything fall down into the void of space. It holds everything together and binds it down by the law of gravity. Skyscrapers, cranes, ants, cars, trees, mountains, oceans, giraffes, humans, sheep — the earth just doesn't let anything fall! Even if a plane takes off or a glider floats in the air, it comes back to ground. So when the universe takes such exemplary care not to let anything fall physically, it won't let anyone fall monetarily either! Rest assured.

Risk-taking pays off not only in the financial sphere but in every aspect of life. It makes your personality blossom and helps you flourish in a holistic way. If you take risks, you are placing your trust in God and the universe rather than ephemeral sources. You declare to the universe that your faith in it is implicit and total. Of course, there is a possibility that it may not always yield a fruitful result. But then, just as we accept night with day, likewise account for the occasional loss or mishap with profit or gain. As they say, it's all part of the package. So throw your insecurities to the wind, take risks and reach out for your dreams — the stars if you so wish, for they're yours for the taking!

4

Maximise — Don't Minimise

Shahrukh Khan once said, "The best financial advice I ever got was from my mother: 'Increase your income rather than cutting your expenses.' That advice has stood me in very good stead throughout my life." The most successful and wealthiest individuals I have ever known or interacted with all follow this principle, whether consciously or unknowingly. They follow the law of increment rather than the law of diminishment. In all that they do, materially or principally, there is a furtherance or onward growth. Once an expense or cost has been established, they take it as a given and think of possible avenues by which they could increase and enhance their resources.

"Maximise; don't minimise" — make that your mantra in life. It's quite logical that when your expenses and outgoings are high, you will stretch your earnings and income potential. Expenses are like energy: the more you release, the more you will have. Consequently, you will stretch yourself. You will optimise your capabilities and make the best of your talents. On the contrary, if your expenses are hardly anything, that generally implies that either you have generous benefactors who foot the bill for everything you do, or you are limiting yourself too much. And if the latter's true, then you really are not making the most of your gifts and capabilities. Always remember that we are all here on this planet to experience life at its gloriest. And that includes, among other things, the greatest material glory that we can aspire towards. The best thing about this universe is its democratic essence. The sunlight is there for everyone to enjoy; likewise with air, water, mountains, woods, flowers, fragrance. The universe gives its bounty freely unto everyone. All it ever desires is that everyone should step forward and stake their rightful claim. The same dictum applies to the material world. The wealth and prosperity is not marked for a select few or monopolised by a chosen clique. It is there for whoever steps forward and stakes their claim. In other words, it is there for all those who make the effort or stretch themselves. So stretch yourself and reach out for the greatest material abundance that the universe proffers — rest assured, there's more apportioned for you than you've ever imagined!

5

Harness All Possible Sources

Our preceding generations scoffed at the very word "loan". To them, it was a dirty four-letter word. They considered it much better to live in penury than "enjoy at other's expense". And probably they were right. The set-up in their day and age demanded frugality: needs were less, resources limited and options even more limited. But times have changed radically. Today, humankind has made tremendous leaps materially, and the sheer plentitude of goods and services is mind-boggling. Though means have stretched, merchandise have outpaced the former. From less than 17 years ago, when there was 1 TV channel, 3 carmakers and 0 luxury boutiques in the country to over 300 channels, 30 carmakers offering 150 variants and almost every top-end luxuy product in the world vying for attention, we have come a long way. Twenty years ago, less than 1 per cent opted for loans to finance their car. Today less 1 per cent pay for their car (whether it's Maruti or Bentley) from their own pocket! And it makes good business sense too. Even if you can afford to buy a Rs 30-lakh car, why would you want to block that money into a depreciating asset? Rather, it's sound economics to make a nominal down payment and invest the remaining money elsewhere.

The Tatas' sensational purchase of Corus Steel in 2007 is a classic example of an entity stretching itself and harnessing all possible sources to accomplish its goal. People often lament they don't have enough money. Even the Tatas could have said that they lack the funds to acquire a company three times its size! And here, we are not talking of a few thousands, lakhs or crores — we are talking of Rs 54,000 crore! How they stretched themselves and created corporate history is a worthy precedent for anyone to follow. They dug their heels deep, crunched the numbers and came up with a bold plan: out of the money required for the acquisition, they strung together 30 per cent from their own pocket and raised the balance 70 per cent through loans from an assortment of Indian and foreign banks. By pulling off the most audacious international corporate takeover in the history of the Indian subcontinent, they proved that where there is a will, there is always a way.

Once you announce a need to the universe, it offers you a medley of sources to be tapped into. Just keep an open attitude and hitchhike at the first available opportunity. No matter what or how much you want, you can always come up with the requisite solution. This example illustrates it best: A friend of mine had a masseur who wanted to buy a piece of land in his native village. He needed three lakh rupees. Now, he had zero savings of his own, and no bank or moneylender would give him money. He did some mental math and came up with a unique idea. He was charging Rs 500 per massage. He went to 15 of his regular clients, most of whom used his services three or four times a month. He proposed to each of them that if they could advance him Rs 20,000, he'd give them 50 massages in a year (while normally in that money they'd get only 40 massages). Now, he was a very good masseur, and all his clients loved him and had implicit faith in him. They all agreed and lent him the money. Within less than a week he bought that land, and that too without initially having even a penny on him! Similarly, if you are enterprising and committed enough, you can put together the resources for your goal, no matter how big or small. The right people will then propitiously come out of the wilderness and make your wildest dreams come true!

6

"It's Within My Reach"

Let's consider an example: If someone is suffering from respiratory ailments, what do they need the most? Fresh air, right? Would it help if they keep staying in claustrophobic surroundings and keep breathing stale air? They have to go outdoors and breathe as much fresh air as possible, exhaling unwanted toxins in the process. Likewise, if a person is down financially, would it help if they retain a tight-fisted mentality? Rather, they have to think big and embrace an "it's within my reach" mentality.

For anything big or small, just have a deep-rooted faith that whatever it is, you can afford it. Whether it's a cruise holiday, a penthouse or a Mercedes, today you might not be able to procure it, but have an unshakeable faith — rather an assurance — that some day you will. Whether you want to buy something or not is a different story, but never say: "Oh that's too expensive!" or "That's out of reach!" By saying so, you send a strong negative signal to the universe. Rather, just say: "I can afford everything." Just by saying that, a surge of confidence would overwhelm you. Automatically, your outlook to everything would undergo a monumental shift. Whether you cook yourself or not, whether you drive yourself or not, it is very comforting to know that you can. Likewise, whether you buy something or not, it will give you a lot of confidence to know that you can. If a 5-carat diamond ring or an Armani suit is what you've been eyeing, rather than being at a conflict between what you want and what you think you can have, just tell yourself that it's yours for the taking. From Olympic champions to top industrialists to statesmen, all those who actually accomplish big feats are the ones who *believe* they can. They are strongly convinced that whatever they want, they can have it. But if you look at them objectively, even they were once normal people. What got them to where they are is an assurance that their dreams are strongly within the gamut of their reach.

As the *Bible* says: "Enlarge the place of your tent. Let the curtains of your habitation be stretched out. Lengthen your cords and strengthen your stake, for soon you will be bursting at the seams!" So, if you realise, even the scriptures tell you the same thing. They tell you that God, too, wants you to live a first-class life, absolutely unfettered and unlimited. Just take the cue and exclaim for everything: "It's within my reach!"

7

The More You Send Out, The More Comes In

Anne Morrow Lindbergh once famously said: "The more one gives, the more one has to give — like milk in the breast!" Also, there is an old saying: "Throw money to attract money!" It is as good a piece of financial advice as you'd ever get! Imagine how it would be if one were to just eat and hog — and not expel! One would bloat to the detriment of one's health. Likewise, if one were to just earn and earn, and not expend, one would just gather an undesirable excess. So expending is as integral to wealth-creation as earning — a simple law of money we all must understand. This paradigm applies to spending as well as giving.

Ponder this: LN Mittal spent (by almost the entire world's standards) an outrageous Rs 250 crore on his daughter Vanisha's wedding in June 2004! Now, if we were to talk from an average person's sense of economics, his wealth should have reduced by that much amount. But, as per *Forbes* figures, his wealth, which stood at $6.2 billion at the beginning of 2004 and before the wedding, quadrupled to a staggering $25 billion towards the end of the year and after the wedding! He went from being the 62nd richest man in the world to the 3rd richest! And, in the interim, he even bought what was then the world's most expensive house in central London for Rs 560 crore! Seems the more he spent, the more his net worth grew! Defies most people's idea of economics, but then, that's the way the ball rolls! The more money you throw, the more you get — simple as that.

The mechanism of money outflow applies most effectively to philanthropy. It's not just a coincidence that the wealthiest people in the world are also the greatest givers — and their wealth-creation never abates. In his book *Start Late, Finish Rich*, David Bach said: "Over the years, I've spent a lot of time studying the rich and the super rich. The more I've learned, the more I've become convinced that most people who achieve great wealth have at least one thing in common — giving!" The man whom *Forbes* magazine has calculated to be the richest person ever in history, John D Rockefeller, was also one of the greatest philanthropists ever. From his very first paycheck, he donated 10 per cent of his earnings to his church. As his wealth grew, so did his giving, primarily to educational and humanitarian causes. Bill Gates went from being the richest person in the world to seeking active retirement from Microsoft and creating the largest charitable foundation in the world — while in the process his personal wealth kept snowballing further. Almost a year after pledging a gargantuan $31 billion to the Bill & Melinda Gates Foundation, Warren Buffet became the wealthiest person in the world. Sir John Templeton, considered to be one of the greatest investors ever, was once asked the secret to his enormous wealth. He replied: "All my life, I have just followed a simple principle: Give more and more will come back to you."

Winston Churchill once said: "We make a living by what we earn, and we make a life by what we give." It's a little ersatz — and somewhat contrary to mathematical principles — but the more you give in life, the more you will see your finances multiply. The "have mores" *always* give more. As the saying goes: "Whoever sows sparingly will also reap sparingly, and whoever sows generously will also reap generously." What goes around comes around, and the more generous you are, the more money will flow to you. And it's not that "wealthy people tend to give" but it's often that "giving people become wealthy". Arjun Sharma, the owner of the iconic Select Citywalk mall in Delhi, once proferred me his insights on wealth: "I believe money is a very small part of wealth. I feel immensely privileged to share my abundance with others. In fact, the less I own, the more the universe gives me back!" No wonder, the universe gave him the best high-street shopping heaven in India!

I was first initiated into the law of giving many years ago when I serendipitously came across Linda Goodman's bestselling book, *Star Signs*. Referring to the law as the Money Mystique, she wrote: "The secret of the Money Mystique is that the green energy of money travels in a magnetic circle. Let go of it, and it follows that invisible circle of pure and powerful energy, infallibly returning to you multiplied, flowing through you and outward in its circular path — and back. There is such a wild sense of euphoria that comes when you realise you're free of the chains that bound you to the green paper called money — when you finally comprehend that the swiftest and surest way to get it is to *give* it. It's FREEDOM!"

Suze Orman in her *Twelve Steps to Wealth* outlines giving as the final step of wealth-creation and offers a practical insight: "One way I know to keep our hearts and hands open is to give money away on a regular basis. How much does one give? I'd say a respectable amount. For someone who is in severe credit card debt, that amount may be $5 a month; for others it may be a lot more. Only you will know the answer to that question. Whom do you give to on a monthly basis? Choose a nonprofit organisation or a place of worship — or you could give to your parents if they need it. You give to make an offering. When you make an offering you feel generous, and when you feel generous you feel powerful, be it the first check you write, or dollar you spend, at the beginning of each month — that way you start each month from a place of generosity and openness, which is the stance of a truly wealthy person."

Giving and receiving are as natural as the rhythm of our breath, in and out, over and over and over again. In all the world's major traditions, giving is an integral concept: daan in Hindusim, tithing in Christianity, tzedakah in Judaism, seva in Sikhism and zakat in Islam. As St Francis of Assissi said: "It is in giving that we receive." We proclaim to the universe that money is just energy, and we are merely conduits for that energy. So, the more we release, the more we get — that's how simple wealth-creation really is!

Chapter Five

HUMANLY

"Life owes us little; we owe it everything. The only true happiness comes from squandering ourselves for a purpose."

— John Mason Brown

1

Bring Home More Sunlight

Family is the cornerstone of human civilisation. Most of us live and endure anything for our family. If you look around, you will find that most people work a lot harder when they have a family to support. If you ask them what is the one thing they would stretch themselves for, their answer would unanimously be: "For our family." Our family is the most abiding and the strongest support system we have. They are the ones who ushered us into this world and made it such a liveable place for us. Our parents taught us how to eat, smile, love, laugh, sing and give; our siblings were the first friends that we ever had and our children are angels in our home who bring us ever closer to God. So it's very important that you give your family your sustained love, attention and involvement.

There's a beautiful saying: "Bring home some sunlight every day." It means that no matter how tough the going, you should transmit the most positive vibes to your family always. If you are leading an exemplary life and have a sunny disposition, your family members will take the cue and follow your example — quite like if one member of a team lifts their standard, the entire team's morale gets lifted and the collective standard rises. Most children emulate their parents' example. We should always remember that whatever we are now creating will have a ripple effect on our children and the coming generation. It will put things in perspective when you realise that your success goes beyond you to your children, grandchildren, great-grandchildren, and so on.

Let every good work begin first and foremost at home. As someone has said: "The part most illuminated is the one right next to the source!" Likewise the people most likely to benefit from our evolution are those closest to us — our loved ones. We owe it to them to make the best that we can of ourselves.

It becomes our sacrosanct duty to work concertedly towards our loved ones' welfare and growth. Springing surprises on them or showering them with gifts (in whatever capacity we can, be it clothes, flowers, chocolates, cards, toys, etc), taking them for outings to the movies, picnics, etc, would contribute immensely to their well-being. Also, make a resolve to keep them away from as much bitterness and angst as you can. Even the busiest and the most successful people on this planet have a common rule: they seldom bring their work home. In other words, they don't bring the stress of their workplace home. Frankly, though nobody deserves to be a recipient of your frustration or work-related stress, the least that does is your family. Give them the best of yourself, and all the sunshine that you can gather. In fact, be like the sun itself that gives so much life and inspiration to each of us. Just imagine, if one sun in the universe can make it so beautiful, how much more beautiful it'd be if there were one "sun" in each household! The potential is there — all we need to do is tap it.

2

Lend a Helping Hand

Leo Tolstoy once said: "The sole meaning of life is to serve humanity." The beauty about human civilisation is that each one of us can be an individual entity, yet we need others for coexistence and evolution. Even if you were to say that you want no help from others, yet there is very little that you'd be able to do on your own, apart from your daily chores. Even if you were perpetually living indoors, yet you'd need electricity to run your fan or light, which is being generated and supplied by a power company run by fellow humans; or even if you were living like a hermit by the light of a lamp, yet you'd need oil to run it (which is being supplied by someone else). To write, you'd need paper and pen (made and supplied by others). Technically, if you look at the micro level, you'd realise that there's *nothing* in today's world that can be done without the support of others. Even if you don't realise it consciously, it is an inviolable truth that we need others in our life. So just like you need others to help you in the conduct of your day-to-day life, they need you too.

Help them as generously as you can. Because this universe is a boomerang. What goes out invariably comes back. By helping others, we send a positive signal to the universe, and it responds by sending the right people to us. They come out of the woodwork, so to say, to take us and our plans forward. Like players on a stage, people start making their entrances at the most opportune time because we've already set forth a wonderful momentum by helping others.

Michael Caine wrote these wonderful lines in the introduction of his book *Acting in Film*: "There's a reason why I'm writing this book. There are many actors who know as much or more than me. But part of this business is more than a business: it's a community. And a community where people share experiences with one another. What I know today is the result of what successful actors have shared with me. I'm just passing on the torch." What an amazing insight into helping others! As Sri Sri Ravi Shankar said: "Human life is a great and rare gift, and all people on this planet should have the chance to express through their lives the full potential of their humanness." We can actually accomplish this wonderful state only if we help others. By helping others, we are actually helping ourselves. By sharing with others, we are effectively creating an apparatus for others to share with us. Someone has beautifully said: "I went out to find a friend but found none there. I went out to be a friend and found that there were friends everywhere!"

Practise this simple exercise to see how sacrosanct others in our life are: Imagine yourself alone on an island. Imagine you have everything else there — food, water, fresh breeze and tranquillity galore; in fact, the most picturesque surroundings — but no human contact. How long do you think you can subsist, much less sustain, in that state? A day, a week, a month, three months! After that, you'd definitely be driven insane. I once saw a documentary about Alaskan outback on National Geographic. It featured a couple who had been living for 17 years with their children in remote wilderness with no signs of civilisation for the next 400 kilometres! This is what the man said: "If something were to happen to my family, I would go back into civilisation the very next day!" Imagine the import of that statement from someone living such a bizarre life! So even if you are a recluse, you need human touch. And since you do, why not ensure that humans are touched by your presence too!

3

Respect Begets Respect

At a fundamental level, every human being wants to feel important. Regardless of what we do or where we come from, the most compelling need in each one of us is to be accorded respect. Respect is a very rudimentary human need. Most people take others for granted and treat them as mere props in their life. But the best amongst us show sensitivity and respect to the rest among us. Someone has rightly said: "The true mark of a man is how he treats his subordinates." The best rulers and statesmen in history have been those who have mustered goodwill rather than fear from their subjects and followers. I have observed that giving others basic respect and courtesies makes it much easier to get any work done. It is very easy to be flippant and rude. But one needs a lot of strength of character to be chaste and respectful to others. I can vouchsafe that the best support I've got anywhere is when I've called someone "Sir" or "Ma'am" and been very polite generally. On the contrary, the toughest times have been if I've ever been abrasive or impolite, or rubbed someone the wrong way. By giving others importance, you demonstrate to them that they are eminent and worthy of attention. Something deep within them feels happy and satiated. The more respectful you are, the more respect you get, and the more worthy you make others feel, the more self-worth you get. As they say: "Do unto others as you'd like them to do unto you." Next time just keep this in mind if you're tempted to prune others to size. Just swap places with them and feel how they would if they were at the receiving end of your bite.

In fact, respecting others should be independent of their age. You could show children you respect them if you give them a patient hearing and let them know that their opinions are significant. Likewise, you could show elders you respect them by soliciting their advice and taking their suggestions. You could show your peers and colleagues you respect them by encouraging their participation in your work and by appreciating their achievements. Many people are generally respectful and agreeable till they are outside their home. They seem very courteous on the face of it. But the moment they come home, they become remonstrative, whether mentally or physically. Their barbs and taunts are enough to scald anyone. One has to realise that the strongest foundation is our home, and the most enduring relationship our association with our spouse. Someone has pertinently said: "A spouse scorned is divinity scorned!" So you must, above all, give your spouse respect by listening to them and cherishing their presence.

As the saying goes: "Like begets like." Only by giving respect will you get it — and, as my experience suggests, there is not a single person in this universe who doesn't want to be respected! By giving respect, one doesn't mean pseudo-politeness. Rather, give genuine respect. It really doesn't take much to demonstrate respect: just a heartfelt gesture, greeting or word often suffices. In fact, most people cause disrespect not by their actions but by their words. Choose your words with discretion and lace them with a genuine concern for humanity, and you will see how people go out of their way to help you in everything.

4

Give More of Yourself

I have seen that those amongst us who give of themselves the most are the ones who enrich humanity the most. I draw from personal experience again. I do numerology counselling, free of charge, purely as a means to help others. At last count, I'd have done numerology for at least 15,000 people and not charged a dime! My take has been, and always will be: if God has given you a gift with which you can help others, then it will be spiritual short-circuitry not to put it to good effect. And I bear testimony to the fact that the more I help others (or at least try to) the more abundance comes into my life. If I were to put a monetary denomination to it, I'd say that if I've helped anyone to the tune of 10 rupees, I've always received 100 rupees back, that too double quick! No hyperbole.

When it comes to helping others, make a pact with yourself that you are not going to withhold, that you're going to stretch yourself as much as you can. I once came across this beautiful message on a greeting card: "Give more of yourself.

In a sense, fill yourself up to fullness, to where you overflow in giving!" In fact, the more you give of yourself, the more you get for yourself.

Today, most people are unhappy not because they don't have enough — it's because they don't *give* enough. Dada Vaswani once said: "It is the measure with which we do something for society that makes us happy." In order to be happy, you have to first make others happy. Give not just of your resources, but also of your time and energy. It would contribute to your growth at a holistic level. When you give, you are in tune with the highest vibrations in the universe and inspire others to an exalted level. An old story illustrates this point. It tells us of a woman travelling alone in the mountains. One day, she discovered a precious stone in a stream and placed the stone in her rugsack. Later, she came upon a man who was hungry. When she opened her sack to share her food with him, the man at once noticed the stone. Realising that it was so valuable that if he sold it, he could live off it for the rest of his life, he asked her for it. She immediately handed it to him, and off he went, smiling at his turn of fortune. A few days later, however, he retraced his steps and returned, stone in hand, to find the woman. "Wise woman," he said, "thank you for the gift of this precious gem — it is indeed extremely valuable. But I am returning it to you with the hope that you will give me an even greater gift. Please give me that which is within you that allowed you to give this stone away to me!" So, when you give of yourself, the spirit with which you serve is by itself the greatest asset the beneficiary of your service can receive and benefit from. While giving, you are propelled not by an acquisitive desire but by an altruistic force, a force that operates at the highest frequency. As someone has rightly observed: "Give rhymes with live; covet rhymes with fret."

Another thing I have noticed with giving: the ones who give the most are those that do it discreetly, without making much noise or ado about it. They do it quietly and unobtrusively. Look at nature: Does a flower make fuss while emanating its fragrance? Does a tree announce before allowing anyone the benefit of its shade? Does a river get offended if anyone in particular drinks at its banks? Does nature change its seasons for only a select few, excluding others from its privilege? Does the moon not emit its radiance for everyone equally? Does the sun not shine for everyone? Does a cow not offer its milk to everyone? So obliterate divisiveness from your life and give heartily of yourself. Your entire personality will flourish and blossom, drawing others to you like bees to honey. Giving of yourself will open doors to your personality which you hitherto didn't even know existed. It will show you vistas which you hadn't even imagined before. Giving of yourself will draw you closer to yourself, to your true identity, which often lies camouflaged in the façade of self-absorption. So give freely and live freely.

5

Like Others to Be Liked

Most of us — rather all of us — love appreciation. To be liked is a universal need. Wanting to be famous, recognised, successful are just variations of that. So when somebody says he or she wants to be famous, what they are essentially saying is that he or she wants to be liked. The happiest people are also, incidentally, liked the most, and vice versa.

Though everybody wants to be liked, how many people actually take the effort to like others? If you carefully observe, most people are perpetually picking on others or finding faults in them. Though it's quite true that some people have annoying habits, yet it's also true that the very same people have positive attributes as well. Yin and Yang, day and night, positive and negative, head and tail can't but coexist. Just like you can drive safely only if you keep your attention on the road and look straight ahead, when dealing with people, you can have harmonious relations only if you focus on their good aspects. Of course, every now and then you also have to look in the rear-view mirror to keep things in perspective, likewise, in your relationship with others also you have to be aware of their shortcomings. But just like you can't let your rear-view sight affect your driving, you shouldn't let other people's shortcomings affect your overall opinion of them. Tempting as it is, avoid being judgemental and subjective. Remember their good points and appreciate them for it. It's akin to how everything else works in this universe — the boomerang effect. The more you like others, the more they will like you.

As Sri Sri Ravi Shankar once said: "Even terrorists are basically good people, as they are willing to put their life behind their cause! They just need the right direction in life." Even Jesus Christ said: "Hate the sin, not the sinner." And as Francois Gautier said: "Flowers grow on their own — all that we can do is water them a little bit!" Likewise, every person eventually fulfils their potential and their destiny. All we have to do is give them that nudge, that encouragement. And the best way to do that is to make them feel loved. Most of us are familiar with the fable of the frog prince and the princess. Just a kiss from the princess transformed the ugly frog into a handsome prince. That's how most people in this world are: intrinsically nice, warm people, maybe a little rough around the edges, but always waiting to be metamorphosed into special entities. All they need is to feel liked and wanted.

And the good news is: it doesn't take much to like people. Just as you like the sun not for its searing heat, but its brilliant light; you like an air conditioner not for its noise but for the cooling it emits; you like money not for its ephemeral nature, but for the comforts it brings you; you like an airplane not for its jerky landing but the ease and speed with which it transports you over great distances, you should like people not for their overbearing characteristics but for their intrinsic humanness. Like them, warts and all, and you will be amazed at how much they will like you in return!

6

Grow in Humility

Guru Ding Le Mei once said: "When we are ready, we are ever in the presence of the Higher Ones, but we must also have eyes to see and hearts of great simplicity to understand." A person without humility is like a bull gone berserk: it has the power and potential, but not the temperance needed to keep its force in check. Likewise with humans: though most of us are capable of great things, yet we need to be mellow and humble in order to accomplish anything worthwhile. "Pride goes before a fall" is a moral we all learnt in school but most sadly left it behind in their textbooks. It is usually ego that keeps anyone away from fulfilment. Humility requires us to surrender to a higher force that is much greater than all our faculties can perceive. It is essentially an acceptance of that force and its all-pervasiveness. In this sense, stretching yourself has a different meaning here: it means stretching yourself beyond yourself. It is the stage where I becomes We, Me becomes Us, Mine becomes Ours. Only if we are humble and simple can we accomplish this wonderful stage. We've all been raised on a diet of comics, and every superhero we know — Superman,

Spiderman, He-Man, Batman, Phantom — has been innately humble. As that immortal line in the movie *Spiderman* says: "With great power comes great responsibility." And with great responsibility comes great humility.

Humility brings with it flexibility and openness. And once you have flexibility — the ultimate characteristic of stretching yourself — you can accomplish anything. You have to transcend your self-imposed limitations. And as a great philosopher has said: "Assuming your limitations is underestimating yourself." So go beyond yourself to find yourself. One has to have a consummate faith in God and his supreme power for abiding humility. As Guru Ding Le Mei has said: "Whoever believes in God at all, believes in an infinite mystery — something which is always a little beyond his consciousness."

A spirit of humility and surrender is very important in order to learn and grow in life. There is an oft-quoted parable worthy of narration here: Once a man went to an enlightened teacher. He said, "I want to be your disciple. Let me tell you what I have learned." He went on to enumerate his qualifications. After he had finished speaking at length, the teacher asked him if he cared for a cup of tea. The man said yes. The teacher began to pour tea from the kettle. Even after the cup was filled to the brim, the teacher continued to pour. The man shouted in confusion, "What are you doing? Can't you see the cup is overflowing?" The teacher looked at him and said, "This is exactly what you are doing. Your cup of knowledge is overflowing. How do you expect me to put any more in it?" So let us all empty our cups every now and then and make room for new insights by cultivating an ongoing spirit of deep humility in life.

7

Commit Yourself to a Greater Cause

Al Gore, the former US vice-president, once memorably said: "We live in an age of consequence, not debate." At a time when ice is melting by the minute in the North and South Poles, and global warming is not just a chapter in geography books but a palpable reality, we need awareness and a commitment to the greater good.

Thankfully, the world is full of people, who are doing much more than lip service. For instance, one look at actor Leonardo di Caprio's website confirms his higher zeal in life. When most people use their websites as mere propaganda tools, Leonardo is much more conscientious. His site is split vertically into two: one half titled "Leonardo" keeps you updated on his movies while the other half titled "Eco-site" is devoted to the environment and offers tips on positive differences anyone can make. Likewise, there are countless others.

The best part is that each one of us can contribute in our own way, big or small, by virtue of money, time, energy, support or anything else to make this world a better place. Just like there are vocations and choices galore in this world, there are causes aplenty to be championed. For a moment, just imagine the effects of global warming. The very fact we call it so implies that it is all-pervasive, transcending the barriers of creed, country and continent. It does not have a locally concentrated impact. Each and every person and entity on this planet reels in its wake. Likewise with economic upswings and downturns. The oil crisis has its ramification on prices all over the world. Every commodity and service gets affected. Likewise with inflation. It spares nothing and no one. The economic crisis in the US affects even a shop owner sitting in Chandni Chowk, whether he realises it or not. Similarly, hunger in Somalia or civic unrest in Chechnya sends far-reaching ripples, whether one realises it or not. The bottomline is that everything in this universe affects everyone, whether one is aware at a conscious level or not. As Jean-Paul Sartre pertinently observed: "Every human endeavour, however singular it seems, involves the whole human race."

With a surfeit of negativity around us, the need of the moment is to contribute as much positivity to the world as we can, in prayer, deed and word. The least we can actually do is to include in our prayers a plea for world peace. It might sound very jejune, but actually if we all can so much as fuse our thoughts with this beautiful desire, it will have a far-reaching effect. Likewise, if we commit ourselves to environmental conservation, by using eco-friendly recyclables, planting trees, opting for alternative energy sources, using fuel-efficient technology, etc, we will be doing a very concerted service to our planet. Whatever we feel an urging for, let's commit ourselves to it and save our wonderful planet for posterity and the beautiful generations to come. We owe it to them.

Donald Trump once said something that has had a lasting impact on me: "People often ask me, 'How do you make billion-dollar deals and finance them with enormous bank loans? How can you sleep at night?' The truth is, it does not matter. What the hell difference does it make? Think about how 3,000 people died in the World Trade Centre — tragic; and how 3,00,000 people died from the tsunami in Asia in 2004 — 100 times more. What does it really matter if you have a big presentation to give to the president of Citibank at 9 am? Problems that may seem big to you really do not matter in the grand scheme of things." What an amazing insight from one of the world's most ambitious men! Bookmark his quote, and next time you're tempted to dwell on your problems, just read it again — it will help you put things in perspective that no matter what your pursuit, there is always a greater goal that merits your attention and a greater cause that needs to be championed.

Chapter Six

PROFESSIONALLY

"The average person puts only 25 per cent of his energy and ability to work. The world takes its hat off to those who put in more than 50 per cent of their capacity and stands on its head for those few-and-far-between souls who devote 100 per cent."

— Andrew Carnegie

1

Devote Yourself to Your Work

Renzo Rosso, the owner of Diesel jeans empire, when asked his motto, replied: "Diesel is not my company — it's my life." Issac Assimov wrote 475 books in his career. I know many people who haven't written as many words in their lifetime! The secret to his prolificity, he said was, "to keep pushing the envelope as much as possible". Georges Simenon, too, authored more than 500 books. He used to write almost 70 pages a day and stretched his vocabulary in various fields to a point where he would never have to use a dictionary so that he could work without interruption. Bach used to write a canata every week, even when he was ill or fatigued, and Mozart produced more than 600 pieces of music in his lifetime. Thomas Edison wrote approximately 3,500 record books and four million pages of notes throughout his working years. Dr E Sreedharan, the MD of Delhi Metro, is a classic example of a person putting more into his work. In a country saddled with bureaucracy and excuses, he has made it his one-point agenda to accomplish his task within deadlines, come hell or high water, and — quite miraculously for India — within budget! Delhi Metro is a shining example of how one man's devotion can galvanise the entire system into efficiency.

When we devote ourselves to our work, it ceases to be a chore. It becomes a pleasure. My wife Ronicka loves photography so much that she can shoot for 12 to 13 hours at a stretch and not get tired! Her secret is that she is devoted to her calling in life and applies herself consummately to her craft. She often says: "With the camera in my hand, I feel overwhelmed by a Godly energy. It's immaterial whether I have to jump a wall, climb a building, sprint a field, plunge into darkness, dangle from a tree or crouch on the floor in pursuit of the shot that I so earnestly want! Time just stops for me then, and I become one with the soul of the universe."

We spoke of the mind, body and spirit in the previous chapters — you will achieve complete bliss only when you fuse all three and bring them into your work. The best in any field see whatever they do as an inseparable part of their being, an extension of their souls. Rather than working, they are expressing themselves. "The most beautiful thing about work is work itself!" said AR Rahman, after becoming the first Indian ever to win a Golden Globe. MF Husain, even at the fabulously grand age of 94, still paints 10 hours a day! I don't think he considers it work. Neither does Zohra Sehgal who even at 97 does theatre with the energy of a teenager! Derek Pringle once said of Sachin Tendulkar, one of the most prolific cricketers of all time: "Plenty are born with talent but few are as driven as Tendulkar to express it in full, and he is as much a product of the net as blessed genes!" He was referring to Sachin's unfailing commitment to net practice even after reaching the very top. Someone has fittingly said: "Little of lasting value comes easily." For that, we have to give a continued and resolute devotion to our work.

When you are devoted to your work, it becomes your connection to the higher force. As Raghu Rai, one of the India's best-known photographers, once said: "Geniuses are not born. They are so because they have connected. But just that one connect is not enough. You have to re-invent, again and again, keep digging. Find more and more. The well is never-ending." But, first of all, you have to find what you love, *really* love. You need to have a burning passion for what you do. Most of us would be daunted at 16-hour days. But not topmost achievers. They don't even realise they are working for such long hours because, to them, work is an automatic reflex, a natural extension of their personality. Nobody who considers their work mechanical can ever be happy and fulfilled. In order to attain fulfilment, devotion is the only key. Swami Paramhansa Yogananda, in his book, *Autobiography of a Yogi*, mentions that there are yogis and Himalayan masters who meditate up to 20 hours a day, with no signs of fatigue whatsoever — likewise, people who love their work are yogis to whom their very craft is meditation. They embody what a mystic once said: "You must lose yourself to find yourself!"

2

Put Several Irons in the Fire

Versatility is one word that I'm most passionate about. I feel there is an incalculable scope in each one of us to do diverse things, and follow differing callings. In my lifetime till now, I have held 12 different professions — author, editor, publisher, photographer, model, actor, numerologist, communication trainer, voice-over artist, columnist, scriptwriter and motivator — and I still want to do a lot more. In fact, as I write this book, I'm preparing to do a short-term filmmaking course! I can vouchsafe from personal experience what enormous satisfaction and evolution all this diversity has given me. I'm so much more contended than I'd have been if I were uni-dimensional or involved in only one career or activity. Then, even in any particular field of activity, I have tried to be versatile. For instance, as a writer, I have written books on topics as diverse as modelling pageants, numerology, photography, wedding planning, short fiction and motivation! As I say all this, however, allow me to put things in perspective. It's not like I claim to be gifted. I attribute my multiple forays solely to the power of stretching. Just my very desire of realising more of myself has enabled me to experience life at a much more expansive level. In whatever you're doing, there is so much more that you still can. For instance, if you're a cook, probably your style of cooking is so distinctive that you might write a cookbook, or you might think of giving cooking lessons. Likewise, if you're a fitness instructor, you might think of making a unique fitness video or writing a fitness book. If you're a furniture designer, you can venture into glassware, perhaps. If you notice, even the best luxury brands no longer limit themselves to just one product. Roberto Cavalli, Christian Dior, Prada, Gucci offer not just apparel, but sunglasses, shoes, bags, watches, accessories. Brands like Versace and Armani have ventured into the hospitality industry with exclusive luxury hotels. Not just that, Versace has even ventured into designing luxury jet interiors! Likewise, Indian couturiers like Rohit Bal and Tarun Tahilini have ventured into event designing, JJ Vallaya has added floral couture to his repertoire, Ravi Bajaj has his own cafetaria, Ankur Batra has diversified into art and interior designing. The world belongs to individuals who stretch themselves both horizontally and vertically and put several irons in the fire rather than just one.

People who do only one thing end up being myopic. Look at actors the world over. The ones who are loved and admired the most are those who portray myriad roles, covering a wide variety and range. Kishor Kumar was a playback singer, actor, lyricist, composer, producer, director and scriptwriter. Akshay Kumar, till he was doing only action, had limited success, but the moment he started doing comedy and drama as well, he catapulted to the status of a superstar. Aamir Khan proved with *Taare Zameen Par* that he is not just a superlative actor but a superb director as well. Hrithik Roshan is as proficient in dancing as he is in emoting, singing or doing action scenes. AR Rahman, one of the greatest Indian music composers of all time, has experimented with every musical instrument and genre and fused it seamlessly in his repertoire. Sachin Tendulkar has almost every stroke and technique in his arsenal: he is as adept in attack, as he is in defence; as belligerent on the on-side as he is on the off! Some of the best artists that I know are as proficient in oil as they are in watercolour. Companies like ITC and Tata do manufacturing with as much finesse as they do hospitality and service! Hotels have presidential suites as well as standard and budget rooms. Someone once said: "Versatility is as much an attitude as a skill." We should incorporate myriad activities into all levels of our life to help us evolve. Versatility gives us the wherewithal for the ever-changing world we inhabit. It helps us make adaptation a part of our daily lives. As you embrace versatility, you'd find yourself drawn to a wide variety of interests, each of which you should award with your attention for a fuller life. You might then find profound truth in this quote my friend had on his work desk: "I want to be the master of one trade, and a Jack of many thereafter." So by all means master one activity, but being a Jack of many isn't a bad idea either!

3

Make Your Passion Your Profession

No matter what your interest, you can always turn it into your vocation. Otto Bettmann, as a child, began gathering prints and illustrations from his father's waste bin, which he then conserved in an old cigar box. As the years passed, his enthusiasm became an obsession, and he began collecting images of all kinds, acquiring, cataloguing and copying them from old books dug up in libraries, attics, basements, even abandoned family albums! His hobby gradually stretched into an archive so huge that it became a point of reference for anyone who had anything to do with photography or illustration. By the time he sold his archive, which fetched him millions of dollars, it consisted of three million photographs and was considered a collection so priceless that it had to be moved into a secret high-security underground mine in Pennsylvania! It is now part of the Bill Gates–owned Corbis Corporation. And look where he started: collecting scraps from waste bins!

As someone has said: "The one voice worth listening to the most is the voice of your heart." Speaking from personal experience again, I was at one time working as an editor with a book-publishing house. A short while later, I joined a photography class after work, purely because I was deeply fascinated by the medium. As luck would have it, four years later, photography became my principal profession, and today I generate much more money and creative satisfaction from it than I would ever have as an editor! So follow your heart, and the moolah will definitely follow. It is not unusual to hear of people in their mid-forties or fifties giving up their cushy jobs and following their true calling. Amrish Puri, one of the most prolific actors India has ever seen — he acted in over 300 films — quit his insurance job at the age of 39 to become a film actor! Golden Globe–nominated filmmaker Shekhar Kapur was a chartered accountant in England who gave up his cushy job, returned to India and directed his first film at the age of 37! Age and background is never a limitation to accomplish your heart's desire or break new ground in your life. In fact, your passion is what your rightful profession should be. If you like knitting, you can give knitting classes. If you like designing table linen, there is always a market waiting to be tapped into. If you like doing fragrant candles, then why not make it your full-fledged profession? If you love shopping and like helping others out too, then why not become a personal shopper? If giving solace to others comes naturally to you, why not become a healer? If you are amazing at chess, and love competing as well, then why not become a professional chess player? If you're a banker who likes to paint miniatures in your free time, and love it much more than your number-crunching job, then why not venture into painting full-time? For all you know, if your heart lies in it, you'd make a far greater success than zombying through a job that's just a chore. Always remember that the only thing between you and your dreams is your own excuses. Sidestep them and proclaim your true passion in life.

4

Time to Switch

Gautam Buddha said: "The only constant in life is change." Most people are unable to grow in life because they apprehend change. Craig Hickman once said: "Change — no other single word so completely captures the essence of contemporary society and its enterprises." Everything is on a rollercoaster today. We must behold change as an opportunity rather than a threat. If something is not working out in your present field, or if you're not finding the drive, why not change it altogether? Agreed, you might find it disconcerting initially, but so long as it's a planned move, it's going to pay you rich dividends in the long run.

People very often hit cul-de-sacs in their professional lives and don't know how to negotiate them. They are always sceptical if a new opportunity is going to work in their favour. Lurking in their mind is a fear: "What about the EMIs?" "What about the children's education?" "What will others say when they get to know that my spouse is contemplating a mid-life career change?" "How can I do something like that!" "I will have to start all over!" All this paranoia acts as a roadblock to progress.

If you're one of those lucky ones who've found their calling at a very young age, great. But if you're among the vast multitude of us who discover it at a later age, even better! Imagine how much experience you'd have accumulated en route. Like Edison, just imagine how many ways you'd have found out *not* to do something! "The beauty about human condition," I read somewhere, "is the ability to make a U-turn no matter where we are." So if you've a 52-year-old corporate lawyer, and you realise that your actual calling is to plan events, who is to say that that's wrong! Who is to stop you from doing that! Should you keep at your dredgery, just because you've been doing it for X number of years? Just because half your life has not been a labour of love, should you waste the remaining half also on a lost cause? No, my friend, life is too priceless for regrets. The moment you have an epiphany that you should be doing something else, act on it. Act with immediacy. As Dr Joe Vitale has said: "The universe likes speed. Don't delay. Don't second-guess. Don't doubt. When the opportunity is there, when the impulse is there, when the intuitive nudge from within is there, act. That's your job. And that's all you have to do!"

Remember, the ultimate power is always in you to perpetrate and sustain change. I feel the greatest malaise affecting most humanity is "alibism": giving incessant excuses for what is or what is not. They keep passing on the buck, never once accepting the onus for their circumstances. Don't be one of them. Get your chin up and face the music, if need be, but at all times play your own tune!

Above all, accept change fundamentally. As Marilyn Ferguson once said: "Being in a world of fluidity, we will fight change;

knowing a world of fluidity, we will cooperate with change." Don't be attached to the comforts of familiarity, and don't be scared of the ramifications either. Once you change, everything else does. As Rumi said: "No mirror ever became iron again; no bread ever became wheat; no ripened grape ever became sour fruit. Mature yourself, and be secure from a change for the worse. Become the light!" So change, and become the light unto yourself and others.

5

Use it Neck Up

Long ago, I read this line somewhere: "Neck down we are limited; neck up we are unlimited!" It was essentially an ode to the power of delegation. If we look at the symbolism, it is actually true — there is only so much that one can do physically. You cannot be at a bank and a grocery store at the same time. Likewise, if you are the managing director of your company, you cannot double up as a watchman as well. If you are an actor, you cannot be the cinematographer and the spot boy, all at the same time. At any given point in time, no matter where you are, you are just a cog — even if the most important one — in the wheel. You need specialists and professionals in every field working at the same time or at different times to accomplish any worthwhile task. The most successful people in any field of activity are those who delegate the tasks they can't do or others can do in much more efficient and economical ways. Any successful designer today has a team of visualisers, merchandisers, illustrators, sales people, publicists, junior designers, tailors, et al, working together to create a brand. If the designer (even if endowed with superhuman talent!) were to do all this, he or she would either have zero output or a very substandard one.

In today's times, delegation is the best way to maximise one's productivity. Imagine a person who, with a modern convenience like washing machine, still chooses to do laundry by hand! In the process, that person is wasting priceless time and energy, which can be freed up for much greater productivity in other areas. The best way to stretch yourself professionally is to build a team of reliable professionals around you. No matter what or how much you can do, there is always a lot that you can't. Delegation covers precisely those aspects. For instance, an F1 driver has to just focus on the race while a team of engineers awaits him at the pit stop to take care of the technical grind of the race. He cannot be racing and changing tyres at the same time!

And if you look at it, it's a good thing we can't do everything all by ourselves. As Robert H Schuller says: "Lucky are those who need others." It helps us stay connected with each other. The universe is so designed that, no matter what you aspire towards, there are always the right people who, when attuned with, can manifest it for you. So, rather than switch off from people, get to know more and more people, and get the right ones to heighten your productivity. The more you value people, the more valuable your own life and output will be.

Always remember that there is something magnificent about every human being. All you need to do is discover that magnificence and cherish it to the hilt. Henry Ford once said: "You can take my factories, burn up my buildings, but give me my people, and I'll build the businesses right back again!" Make people feel special, and there is nothing they won't build right back for you!

6

Value Your Work

The reason most people don't make their lives valuable is that they don't value their work. They are beset with the notion that other people are doing more significant jobs. But the fact of the matter is that only those people who believe they are doing anything of significance are actually making a worthwhile contribution to the world. You must be familiar with this quote from Martin Luther King: "If a man is to be called a street sweeper, he should sweep streets like Michelangelo painted, or Beethoven composed music or Shakespeare wrote poetry. He should sweep streets so well that all the hosts of heaven and earth will pause to say, here lived a great street sweeper who did his job well." Yes, if there's something else that you feel that you can do better, by all means go for it, lock, stock and barrel. But if there's nothing else that you can think of, then treat your present work with respect. As I've said throughout the book: "If *you* don't, then who else will!" Rather than focusing on the negatives, why not enumerate a list of the positives? I'm sure we can all come up with virtues aplenty. For example, if you are a billboard-painter, those would be:

- I'm doing something that affords visual pleasure to others.
- There are not too many overheads involved.
- I'm an artist whose work is being seen and appreciated by thousands every day.

One can look for positives in everything. Rather, it's not that one can, it's that one *must*! People who attain mastery in their chosen professions are those who immensely like their work. They cherish the sunny aspects of their work and embrace the occupational hazards with equal finesse. Rather than a litany of complaints, they have only the good things about their work to share with everybody. Even if you are a policeman on beat patrol, just think about how much your sheer presence is contributing to the maintenance of law and order in your locality. Even if others don't thank you, you thank yourself and your work for all the good that there is. Van Gogh sold only one work in his lifetime. Still he did not get dismayed and give up what he loved to do. He kept plodding and delving into his craft ever so deeper. A Van Gogh could never have been Van Gogh if he himself did not realise how unique it is to be Van Gogh! Appreciation is important but it is not all. If you find yourself in a situation where your effort is not being recognised the way you'd like to, don't be disheartened. The biggest service you can do yourself when the chips are down is to keep your morale and self-esteem high. When Renzo Rosso, the creator of Diesel Jeans, initially went to stores in New York to sell his merchandise, people laughed at him and sneered how he could even thing of selling his "torn" jeans at such upscale tony stores. However, he persisted and eventually carved Diesel jeans into a multi-million-dollar empire. The bottom line is he valued his work and persisted with it even in the face of ridicule and mockery. MF Husain used to paint billboards and movie posters. He later said that he valued his work of that time as much as he does now when he paints million-dollar paintings. Naseeruddin Shah values his theatre work as much as he enjoys his film work. Only if you value your work and do it with diligence will you actually excel at subsequent higher levels. You cannot think of competing in Olympics if you haven't first earned your spurs in domestic, club-level matches. You can't play international cricket unless you first play club-cricket and then Ranji matches. Regardless of what level of accomplishment you're at, value your work thoroughly, and then watch the magic unfold.

It has been said that during the life of Krishna, only three knew of his essence; only twelve recognised the Christ; and very few recognised the Buddha! However, that didn't stop them from being who they were or what they were doing! So nothing should stop us either. Let us all cherish our unique individuality and value our work thoroughly — for work truly is worship.

7

Aim for the Stars

Leo Burnett, the advertising moghul, once said: "If you reach for the stars, and fall, you will get the moon. But if you just reach for the tree branch, and fall, you will end up in the mud!" So, set your benchmark very high. Only if you aim for the very best, will you grow to your true potential. The very foundation of stretching yourself is based on the premise of growth and the quest for excellence. Tell yourself that the only way is the way of excellence. If you're a sportsperson, then every time you play, give it your best shot. Honestly speaking, most people are focused on just the end result. It's the journey that counts too.

No matter what you do, always keep in mind the recipient of your service. Put yourself in their shoes. If you were them, wouldn't you want to get the best out of you? The best institutions and individuals epitomise superlative standards to one and all. A flower gives its fragrance regardless of who gets it, and the sun emits its light regardless of who gets illuminated. That's because it's their very nature to do so. Likewise, you should deliver excellence regardless of who your customers and beneficiaries are. Chances are if you're committed to excellence, the best customers or patrons will get drawn to you like iron filings to a magnet. Excellence generates a dynamism that's contagious. Strive to be the very best that you can ever be, and honestly there's no limit to that. As Craig Hickman and Michael Silva wrote in *Creating Excellence*: "No matter what all the surveys, studies and comparative statistics indicate, the real race for excellence is the one you run against yourself."

Excellence must be honoured — or rather demanded — in every human activity. As John Gardner once said: "An excellent plumber is infinitely more admirable than an incompetent philosopher. The society which scorns excellence in plumbing because plumbing is a humble activity and tolerates shoddiness in philosophy because it is an exalted activity will have neither good plumbing nor good philosophy. Neither its pipes nor its theories will hold water!" So aim for excellence in whatever you do.

Once you're used to being your best, excellence will become an automatic reflex. You will no longer have to consciously strive for it. Excellence is a desirable quality not just in your workplace but also in every single aspect of your life: health, relationships, lifestyle, personal conduct, goals, etc. It is to be measured not just as a yardstick, but as a philosophy, as a way of life. In fact, excellence is like an opiate — once you get used to it, it is addictive. And, like a mighty magnet, it begins to attract the right resources and people for its attainment. Everything, from your attitude to your surroundings, should exude the quest to excel. You should look like a winner inside out. The one who wins a race of any kind, is the one who is willing to go the extra yard to prepare and then perform. Be equal to the task of preparation, and you will reap immeasurable benefits. Excellence has such amazing spin-offs that one stands truly humbled in its presence. It turbocharges you, leaving you with an intense personal magnetism. Human psyche is such that everybody loves a winner. Don't be just an onlooker, gawking at the victor. Go out there and be one yourself.

Chapter Seven

PERSONALLY

"There are two ways to live your life: One as though nothing is a miracle. The other as though everything is a miracle."

— Albert Einstein

1

Dream Big

Bill Zanker once said: "What you dream about is what you will become. If you cannot even dream of doing big things, you will never do anything big in life." The starting point of all achievement is a dream. An intense, burning, all-consuming dream. So dream big, really, *really* big, for as someone has said: "We are eventually measured by the size of our dreams!"

After winning the best actress Oscar for *The Reader*, Kate Winslet revealed in her acceptance speech how, as an eight-year-old, she had practised her Oscar-winning moments, staring into the bathroom mirror and pretending that the shampoo bottle was an Oscar statuette. It took her 25 years and five losses to eventually fulfil her dream, but she never once stopped dreaming. She said: "Keep dreaming. Because I'm living proof that they can come true. I swear to you, I promise you, that mine is a dream come true!"

I recently read about Jason McElwain, an old autistic high school boy in the US. His father had no hope in him even attending regular school. But fortuitously Jason got through. He was very fond of basketball and nurtured the dream of playing in his school team on a big stage. He was so committed to his dream that he would just stand for hours by the side of the basketball court. Gradually, he started collecting balls from the side and handing them to the coach. After a few years, given his dedication, and the fact that he spent six hours every day at the courts, he was made the junior coach of the team. But in his heart of hearts, he just dreamt to play. Then, one day, in the final game of his coach's career — in the final game of the inter-school championship too — he decided to reward Jason in the last four minutes and help him fulfil his dream. Enter Jason. His first shot was way off the mark as was the second. But what followed was a sheer spectacle. His next six shots were all three pointers shot from the halfway mark, all dunked in the final three minutes of the game, clinching his team the match comprehensively. He instantly became a national celebrity, and people like George Bush and Magic Johnson personally went to meet him. A book on his life was written and a movie scripted as well. When Larry King asked Jason, who hadn't even learnt how to speak till he was five, how he did it, he said: "It was simple. *This is all that I ever dreamt of!*"

Martin Luther King said, "I have a dream" and mobilised millions of Americans in the civil rights movement. The youngest man ever to receive the Nobel Peace Prize, he dreamt of ending racial segregation in the US through non-violent means — and made it possible. Likewise, we Indians owe our independence to countless freedom fighters — Mahatma Gandhi, Rani Jhansi, Annie Besant, Bal Gangadhar Tilak, Bhagat Singh, Chandrashekhar Azad, Subhash Chandra Bose, Sarojini Naidu, Lala Lajpat Rai — each of whom dreamt of liberation from the colonial powers with great intensity and belief and made it a reality one day.

The most important ingredient for success is a dream — the burning, impelling force inside you. A dream when harnessed is power. The first rule of stretching yourself is to dream intensely. Rather than wishing vainfully, dream vividly. After winning the historic Chennai Test match against England, Yuvraj Singh said: "I always dreamt that one day I'm going to win a Test match alongside Sachin Tendulkar (who was his partner at the other end), and now I've done that!"

Someone has rightly said: "There are no great people, only great dreams!" When you choose a dream, that dream will eventually decide your destiny. So choose your dreams wisely and give them your best*est* shot.

2

Set Lofty Goals

It's very important to have lofty goals in life and the wherewithal to go after them hammer and tongs. In 2002, I set my sights firmly on the Grasim Mr India contest. At that time I was an editor with HarperCollins Publishers. My work would typically end at 8 in the night, after which I would go to the gym, work out till 11, get home by midnight, cook my own meal and eat by 1, read some, sleep by 2 and wake up at 7 for the next day in office. I followed this manic routine for six months, during which I pushed myself as far as I could, farther every day. Today, as I look back, I realise that I could pull it off only because I had a goal: to be in the Top 3. I stretched myself optimally, and it paid off. Out of 15,000 participants, I stood second. In retrospect, I wish I had kept my goal loftier: to win the contest rather than be content with a Top 3 finish!

Goal setting is something that has come very naturally to me. While growing up, I had this game which I created in my mind: if I was walking on the road and somebody was coming from the opposite side, I would mentally pick a point (say a pole, a car or a line) between us and challenge myself that if I crossed that point before that person, I'd certainly accomplish whatever goal I had at that point in my life (erudite things like coming in the school's merit list or crazy things like impressing a girl!) or, if I were writing an essay, I would give myself say five minutes by the watch and promise myself the fruition of my goals if I accomplished it in time. This game was an obsession my growing up years and eventually it seeped into my subconscious so emphatically that, even today, setting myself a new goal or challenge or stretching myself comes very naturally, and gives me unspeakable energy. I strongly suggest you create something similar for yourself. The results might not be immediate but eventually you'd be amazed by what you will become. Try it: *it works*!

GE's motto was to be No 1 or No 2 in every market in the world in every service they were rendering. They pursued that goal relentlessly and accomplished it unfailingly. Almost every champion and ace performer has very lofty goals. An ever-exalted benchmark is what spurs them towards an ongoing growth. For a mountaineer, the only worthwhile goal can be to scale the highest summit. What good would it be to be content reaching only the base camp or to aim only at the mid-peak! Similarly, for an athlete or a race driver, the aim is incomplete if it's not for the finish line. What good is it to just go off the starting blocks and aim only for halfway! For an Olympian, the loftiest goal would be to win the gold medal. What good would it be to just aim for a place in the finals! Likewise, every person has to aim for the highest of and for themselves. It's a cardinal sin to be content with mediocrity and half measures. Set the bar really, *really* high and stretch yourself to pip it like only you can!

3

Keep On Keeping On

Roger Bannister once said: "The man who can drive himself further once the effort gets painful is the man who will win." One can say that what oxygen is to air, persistence is to success. It is one of the most fundamental aspects of stretching yourself. Thomas Alva Edison could have stopped at 1 experiment or at 1,000 — but he didn't! He stretched himself to a point where he was eventually successful, even if it meant 10,000 experiments! He then sweated through a further 50,000 experiments to perfect the alkaline battery and took 52 years to perfect the phonograph! When asked his secret, he asserted: "Genius is 1 per cent inspiration and 99 per cent perspiration." Orville and Wilbur Wright tried to fly a thousand times yet failed. But they never abandoned their endeavour. The title of one of my favourite books very interestingly reads: *Success is Never Ending, Failure is Never Final*! How true it is, and how wonderfully it shows us the importance of persistence. In any sport, it so happens that the team that wins is the one that refuses to throw in the towel and battles against all odds. JK Rowling (today the world's wealthiest author) was once on welfare, raising her little daughter all by herself. After working for five years on an old manual typewriter (and writing in an assortment of cafes, and whenever she could get her daughter to fall asleep), she submitted her *Harry Potter* manuscript for publication. Submission after submission proved futile, and the manuscript was rejected 12 times! A reviewing editor even told her to get a day job since he felt that she had little, if any, chance of making money! But she did not give up. Eventually, she got 13th time lucky. And today, she has become the first billionaire writer in the world! All thanks to — the power of persistence. Kiran Mazumdar Shaw was refused a bank loan seven times on the pretext that she was a woman entrepreneur. Unfazed, she put together her own capital of Rs 10,000 and started out with two employees in her garage. Today, within three decades, as the chairperson of Biocon, she has become India's richest woman with a turnover of Rs 2,100 crore. Similarly, Sabeer Bhatia was turned down by 19 venture capitalists before Draper Fisher Jurvetson agreed to give funding to start Hotmail. After winning the prestigious Booker Prize in 2008 for his debut novel, *The White Tiger*, this is what Aravind Adiga said: "I hope all young and first-time writers, who, like me, have been rejected and rejected and rejected will take heart from this and try again. One must never quit."

Persistence could be for anything: pursuing the person you love, following up on an idea, accomplishing a goal you cherish or changing a personal habit. For some, giving up alcohol or cigarettes requires as much persistence as let's say making a million dollars for others. Most people don't accomplish their dreams because they throw in the towel easily. With persistence, you can achieve any glory or any height you wish to scale. Be bullheaded about your goals and life and never accept defeat.

I think the reason most of us read about the spider and King Bruce in our elementary class is for us to learn about life's greatest lesson: try, try, try again and, one day, the victory shall be yours. Imagine, if you are not able to drive well one day, you don't stop driving altogether! If your stomach is unwell, you don't stop eating! If your breathing is irregular, you don't stop breathing! If your body is hurting, you don't just discard it! If your children are misbehaving, you don't leave them on the street! Ditto with your life and aspirations. Just because you've suffered one setback doesn't mean you abort your dreams. Just because somebody's been unfair to you doesn't mean you give up your faith in the goodness of humanity. Just because one of your targets wasn't met doesn't mean that you give up your goals forever. In this age of instant gratification, the world still belongs to people who are in it for the long haul, unmoved and unaffected by short-term losses or gains, setbacks or triumphs. As Alexis Carrel, a Nobel Prize–winning physiologist, once said: "Life leaps like a geyser for those who drill through the rock of inertia."

One of the most legendary books of all time, *The Alchemist*, sold only 900 copies in its first edition, and the publisher decided not to reprint it. But the author, Paulo Coelho, did not surrender his dream: he took it to another publishing house and, as they say, the rest is history. The book soon became a global phenomenon, was translated into 61 languages and became one of the best-selling books in history! *Slumdog Millionaire* ran out of funds while filming, some of its key technicians left before shooting was over, and it was going to have a restricted, straight-to-DVD release. But the cast and crew's collective persistence overcame all odds, the film biltzkrieged the global box-office and eventually won eight Oscars! When

Napoleon Hill interviewed 500 of the most successful people in America, he found out that they all had one thing in common: their greatest success came just one step beyond defeat. They succeeded because they persevered. Or, as someone has said: "They kept on keeping on!"

4

"I Can Do Anything"

Walt Disney once said: "The secret of making dreams come true can be summarised in 4Cs: curiosity, confidence, courage and constancy, and the greatest of these is confidence!" One of the biggest facilitators on the path of evolution is self-confidence. It's very important to have an "I can do anything" spirit. Stretch yourself into the most confident you can ever be and watch the magic unfold. The most fulfilled people that I've ever met are the ones who are self-assured, the ones most comfortable in their skin. They exude a power so strong, so unflappable that it seems as if nothing can shake them. Someone had aptly said once: "People doubt their capabilities, not their weaknesses!" Don't be a Doubting Thomas, embracing your weaknesses and underplaying your strengths. While it is important to rectify your weaknesses, the most important ingredient of confidence is the identification of your unique strengths and capabilities and to build on them. Play up your plusses, and you will automatically feel confident and strong.

Again, confidence, like most other aspects of stretching yourself, is an intrinsic process, an "inside job". It is a sublime quality — if it's in your face, then it could become arrogance. It has to be internally driven. Most people attribute confidence to a cosmetic process. They think appearance or symbols govern confidence and that it is dependant on what car you drive, what brands you wear and what circle you move around in. While all this does have a bearing on confidence, yet that's not what true confidence is about. It's about that core, radiant personality that is independent and mutually exclusive of symbols — a personality that shines through whether you are in a rundown tenement or in a posh villa; that attracts regardless of whether you're attired in street wear or designer wear; that rivets regardless of the dialect and language you are speaking in — in fact, that enchants regardless of whether you're speaking or not! I often humbly tell my friends: "When I had nothing, all that I had was confidence, and today when I have everything, all that I have is confidence." In order to build confidence, one just has to be in touch with one's inner core, that inner voice that is all-powerful. Shut out the noises from the outer world and swim deep into the infinite reservoir of abundance within you. Self-trust is very important in life. Mark Twain once said: "A man cannot be comfortable without his own approval." Just like your body is priceless, likewise your inner worth is incalculable, all-important. Nurture it with all your might and reap benefits that you've hitherto not even imagined.

5

Expect More

Someone has pertinently said: "If it's expected, it will occur!" The reason some people get more out of life is that they *expect* more out of life. Or rather that they expect the most out of life. Unlike some who believe that life wouldn't offer them anything, the topmost performers believe that life would offer them the very best. They expect that the very best things are going to happen to them; they expect universal abundance to unfold unto them. And, magically, that's exactly how is happens. It's quite like going to a restaurant and expecting superb food. You'd call that sort of expectation perfectly logical and rational, right? But what if you go expecting substandard food and service? Then an "anything goes" mindset would prevail, and that's exactly what you'd get. Because you don't mind the abysmal standards. In fact, that's what you've gone expecting!

Just like you expect more out of your surroundings and your environment, expect more out of your life as well. Expect more out of yourself. Think that you deserve a lot better.

That you are capable of a lot more. That everything is of the best*est* standards possible. Expect that all your dreams are being manifested, and all your goals are reaching fruition. Expect that you are happy and all those around you are happy. Expect that only the very best is coming your way. Expect that people are going out of their way to help you. Expect that the universe and all its creations are opening up to you. Expect that you are God's favourite child and that he wants the best life for you. Expect complete harmony and order and alignment in all that you do, think, feel and experience. Always remember that your life will be in direct proportion with your expectations. Agreed that sometimes you might be let down, sometimes you might have to face hurdles, sometimes you might have to undergo duress, sometimes you might not get your due, but do not be dismayed. Come what may, never lower your expectations. Always expect the tide to turn in your favour. Always expect largesse. Always expect more. If *you* don't, then who will!

It is by God's grace alone that any of us can achieve anything. However, we are the instruments through which his grace flows. We need to expect, not in a wishy-washy manner but with a firmness of mind that whatever we desire shall come to pass. Psychologists have long proven the healing effects of expectation. Even chronically ill patients, when administered placebo without their knowledge, but told it's a drug, get healed. How? Because of the powerful force of expectation. They expect that just because they've been given a medicine, they will get healed. And so they do, but not due to any physiological remedy. But because of the mountain-moving magic of expectation. Ben Sweetland once said: "The world is full of abundance and opportunity, but far too many people come to the fountain of life with a sieve instead of a tank car, a teaspoon instead of a steam shovel. They expect little, and as a result they get little!" So, expect the very best, and rest assured that it shall providentially come to pass.

6

Act NOW

Sunil Bharti Mittal once said: "If you're caught between speed and perfection, always choose speed, and perfection will follow!" Whenever you get the impulse to do something substantive in life, just follow it instantly. Most human productivity goes waste solely because people dilly-dally. Procrastination is the bane of productivity. Centuries ago, Kabir advised us: "Whatever you're going to do tomorrow, do today; whatever you are going to do today, do now. Calamity strikes in a moment — what will you do then?"

Most people are inhabitants of future. They keep waiting for the opportune time, sometimes interminably. Their plans are deferred more than they are fructified. Gradually, in their anticipation for the "perfect" time, the drive peters out, and they eventually lose the initiative. Acting with immediacy, with a swiftness of purpose, is the only way to accomplish anything worthwhile. Agreed, the action might take long to bear fruit, but at least you'd have done your bit. Whatever you do, make the present moment your priority. It is only in the here and now that you can do anything substantial. The ones who accomplish the most are the ones who go for it *the moment* there is an opportunity. They don't keep sitting on their haunches, waiting for it all to come together. Honestly, it's seldom the perfect time! Something or the other will always be found wanting. As they say: "Don't miss the sky for the stars!" Make an objective assessment of what you have, draw up a plan and then go at it, hammer and tongs. By acting with immediacy, you get the headstart and the beginner's advantage.

In chapter 1, sub-chapter 2, "Be an Idea Miner", we mentioned how JK Rowling, Sylvester Stallone and Jaideep Sahni got the ideas respectively for *Harry Potter*, *Rocky* and *Chak De India*. It's very important to note why these ideas became such thumping successes — it's because these people believed in their ideas and followed them through instantly: JK Rowling started writing *Harry Potter* as soon as she got back to her flat after the train journey from Manchester to London. Sylvester Stallone started writing *Rocky* the very day he saw the news clip about the championship fight. Likewise with Jaideep Sahni — he started penning the script of *Chak De India* immediately after reading the newspaper story about the Indian women's hockey team.

My first book, *Model Dreams*, was written similarly. Immediately after Grasim Mr India, I was at a party when a young guy came up to me and asked me how he should prepare for the contest, and if there was any material/manual that he should peruse. That set me thinking. What if there were a book that took prospective contestants through the motions of preparing for the pageant! That very night I got back home and started writing. Within four months, that book was born. Etienne Mabillier once said: "I expect to pass a way but once — any good therefore that I can do, let me do it now. Let me not defer or neglect it, for I shall not pass this way again!" Deepak Chopra has a very beautiful insight too: "The past is history, the future is mystery, and this moment is a gift. That's why it's called the present!" Wonderful. So let's all bring our "presents" into play and optimise their potential. Whatever we want to do, let's set the momentum *now* by acting with lightning immediacy. As Johann Von Goethe has said: "Whatever you can do or dream you can, begin it. Boldness has power and magic in it, begin it now."

7

Live Forward, Not Backward

The world belongs to those who don't rest on laurels or accomplishments. If one were to do that, one would atrophy. Rather, every day you should feel that you're starting afresh, that you have to create something new. As someone wisely said: "A stone that doesn't roll, gathers moss."

Most people lug the baggage of their past wherever they go. No wonder they are so enervated and weighed down. Scaling heights and travelling into the future implies being light and unfettered. So, in your quest for a beautiful future, first of all embrace the present and let go of the past. Reaching out for the future doesn't mean forsaking your past — rather it implies befriending it. Most people are morbidly attached to the past and continually harp about how it used to be in the "good old days". They gladly succumb to their memories, yearning for what was, and being oblivious to what *is*. Besides, most people lug bitterness and angst with them throughout their lives. A very important aspect of moving forward is forgiveness. Let's consider an example here: if somebody's suffering from food poisoning, they will not be well unless the toxins have been purged from their system and their body has been cleansed. Likewise, if you've had a bad experience or somebody's been mean to you, you won't be happy unless you make peace with it and move on. Only by sublimating past foulness into forgiveness will you surge harmoniously forward in life.

Everybody has a past, a history that is saddled with not-so-pleasant instances. The sensible thing is to go beyond those unpleasant memories. Just let go — like a heavy weight just let it drop. As Sandee Corshen once said: "You cannot deal with today if yesterday is staring you in the face!" The moment you choose to release your past from your consciousness, you will experience a wondrous power. You will open yourself up to the largesse of the universe, and all the cosmic abundance that was meant for you will now come your way.

An important part of reaching out for the future is embracing change and the transformation it brings. Reach out fearlessly and boldly, secure in the knowledge that whatever happens, happens for the best. Reach out for the stars, knowing that the ground beneath your feet is secure and solid. Reach out fully, not half-heartedly. Remove barriers of the past from your mind. Make room for only the present and the very promising future. And always remember what Joel Osteen once said: "Our greatest day lies ahead, not behind!"

8

Be a Self-starter

Tony Robbins once said: "If you want to make it big, you've got to push yourself beyond your limits. You've got to pump yourself up and get yourself into a hyper mental state. And you have to do this yourself. Nobody else can do this for you." The most successful people amongst us are self-starters, the ones with initiative. They don't wait for that nudge or motivation from others. They set their own goals and their own objectives. Their yardsticks are self-defined and independent of external forces.

As a self-starter, you will be propelled by your own steam. You will reach as high as you aspire and as far as you desire. But since nobody will take you by your finger, you will have to initiate it yourself. And, at the end of it, if you look at the benefits, they are enormous: you will be your own Leonardo da Vinci, the creator of your own creation. If your life and your goals are coloured by others' aspirations, then how will your individuality get expressed? Each one of us is here on this planet to express our life force, our spiritual blueprint. When you are a self-starter, regardless of how much or how little you accomplish, there will always be the satisfaction that your success is yours and yours alone. You will be dancing to your own music, which is the sweetest. "A journey of a thousand miles starts with a single step", it is said, and a person with initiative has the wherewithal and conviction to take that step. They are neither afraid to fail nor daunted to fall. There is a sense of confidence and a surety of purpose in them.

Rachel Reuben once said: "Growth is an organic process. Once you start something, it will invariably lead you somewhere." The important thing is to start. Once you set the ball rolling, the momentum picks up by itself. But the important thing is for you to put it into motion. Don't wait for others to lead you or show you the way — rather, *you* create the way! If you're not being able to see the light, then light your own torch and find the way. As Paulo Coelho has said: "You cannot judge the beauty of a particular path just by looking at the gate!" Whatever you want to do, at least initiate the process. You'll be amazed how all the resources start getting magnetised to you. Right people will get drawn, right opportunities will come by, right channels will open, right markets will get tapped. If let's say you have to go from Delhi to Chandigarh, unless you get into your vehicle, and initiate the process, how will you get there? Likewise with life. The distance between you and your dreams is determined only by you. The longer you procrastinate, the more the distance increases. So the moment you get the impulse, or the nudge from within to pursue an idea or a dream, act on it. Seize the initiative and go for it. Only you can do it. It has been rightly said: "Some people may have greatness thrust upon them, but nobody has excellence thrust upon them!" You have to achieve it yourself, through initiative, conviction and tenacity of purpose and, as Donald Trump says, by constantly "plugging in to your own electricity".

9

Embrace Your Failures

What would day be without night? Or what would alpha be without omega? What would victory be without struggle? Incomplete, right! Likewise what would a wonderful life be without a fair share of setbacks? I once got this wonderful SMS: "You first learnt to walk after falling down thousands of times. Thank God you didn't take every fall as some personal flaw — or you'd still be riding around in a pram!" So, never denounce your failures. Even the mistakes you might have committed, inadvertently or not, are all part of the learning curve. General Johnson, Johnson & Johnson's founder, once famously said: "If I wasn't making mistakes, I wasn't making decisions!" Keep in mind that there is nothing undesirable in the universe. Everything that happens carries with it the seed of opportunity. Your biggest failures contain your biggest growth potential.

The thing with many people is that they are so fixated on success that they forget that one of its biggest components is failure! They are so fixated on the destination that they forget to enjoy the journey. And no journey, regardless of the mode of travel, is ever complete without the odd bump, jerk or speed breaker. Learn to cherish your failures. Learn to learn from them. Even the moon has fault lines and craters. Each one of us has their flaws. While it is important not to overlook them, yet it is equally pertinent not to despise them either. Have a healthy acceptance of your faults and then work on them objectively. Encourage inputs from your well-wishers and then take corrective measures. The key to stretching yourself as a person is to first stretch your acceptance of yourself. And that can happen only when you see a composite picture, not just the rosy tint. Life is meant to be lived first-hand, not through extension. And committing mistakes is an integral part of growth. As an ancient Tibetan master once said: "What I may merely tell you, you will neither believe nor understand. The art of learning is to prove things for yourself. What you find for yourself, you will never efface from your memory." Even if what you find is discordant with what you were aspiring towards, take heart. Your mistakes, like your triumphs, are your own. Don't abdicate them. Let's consider an analogy: Someone has two children. One is outstanding and the other unruly. The parents just don't discard or disown the second one. They try and make him or her see sense. That can happen only when the errant one is embraced. But by rebuke or censure, the child might worsen.

Embracing mistakes, however, doesn't imply a licence to repeat them in future. The very moral of mistakes is that one learns from them rather then ignoring them. You go to the next level only by clearing the present one — and that will happen only when you learn your lessons well. As Abraham Lincoln once said: "My great concern is not whether you have failed, but whether you are content with your failure!"

Own your personality in its entirety, and there will be no divisiveness left. If you want only the daylight, then you are looking at half the picture. The night has its own purpose: it is there so you can sleep and recoup your energies, starting out on a fresh note. Likewise, the failures are there so that you can re-strategise and start afresh, wiser and more evolved from the experience. Always remember the wise words of Benjamin Franklin: "Those things that hurt, instruct!" And if you still need further substantiation, take heart from the fact that Albert Einstein — probably one of the greatest geniuses the world has ever known — failed his first university entrance exam at the age of 17! However, he embraced his failure, learnt from it and became the indefatigable wizard that the world came to know him as. So, embrace your failures, learn from them and keep incessantly working towards the genius that's latent in all of you.

10

Patience Pays

Joel Osteen once said: "God works the most when we see it the least." We live in times of instant gratification. Whether it's at work or in personal relationships, most people want to see results right away. They are just not prepared to wait. But that's not how God works. Wise ones have always said: "There is a time and a place for everything under the sun." The sooner we understand that there is an appointed time for everything, the easier it will be for us. It's quite like saying a plane takes off from Delhi at 9 am, and it's scheduled to land in Mumbai at 11 am — it can't land any faster just because you are edgy or can't wait! Besides, if there's congestion in the air traffic, or due to inclement weather, it could even extend beyond it's scheduled arrival time. These things are beyond anybody's control and your getting impatient isn't going to make it land any faster. It will land when it has to, period!

At any stage in life, there are only two attitudes that you can demonstrate: a good one or a grumpy one. Likewise with patience. You can either trust God and stay cheerful, assured that victory is in sight or you can sulk and spite God, riling that things never go your way.

Learn from nature. Seasons change but imperceptibly. Night segues into day but gradually. A caterpillar metamorphoses into a butterfly but not suddenly. A baby turns into an adult but slowly. Snow melts but slowly. A seed matures into a fruit slowly. A bud blossoms into a flower slowly. Likewise with our goals and dreams. There is always a gestation period between aspiring towards something and getting that.

In the interim, you can either be at peace or at conflict — the choice is yours. The former can be liberating and the latter enslaving. Always be at guard against two Fs — force and frustration — and cultivate two Ps — peace and patience.

Whether it's your goals or something in your personal life, you must learn to trust God's timing — that, in due course, it shall come to pass. Some people dismiss this line of thinking as fatalist, saying: "If it has to happen in its own time why bother, why put in the effort!" But again I'd say, that's not how it works. You must endeavour for everything — only the timing and the end result are not in your control. But till then, your efforts should not flag. Patience does not imply passivity; rather, it demands persistence.

I think many of us have read about the Chinese bamboo tree — for five years they keep watering it but it doesn't grow even a single inch and then, suddenly, within six weeks, it grows to a height of 90 feet! Now, do you think the tree would have grown if they hadn't watered and fertilised it all these years? No way! Likewise, just keep doing your bit in life. You never know when the tide will turn in your favour. It might happen today, tomorrow, next month, a year or a decade later. But turn it will, one day for sure. Till then just relax and let it happen in its own sweet time. Carve the groove of patience firmly into your mind. As someone has beautifully said: "God answers prayers in three ways — he says yes and gives you what you want; he says no and gives you something better; he says wait and gives you the best in his own sweet time!" So wait, and be prepared for the very best to come into your life — but at God's appointed time!

11

Dare to Be

It may be emphatically said that courage is the leitmotif of accomplishment. Everything noteworthy needs courage. Courage is nothing but stretching beyond fear. Courage is not the absence of fear but the transcendence of it. I once got a beautiful message in a fortune cookie: "Courage is fear holding on a minute longer!" Actually, in anything you ever do, you have to consciously choose between courage and fear. So, technically, every time you don't choose courage, you are choosing fear! Courage will make you take decisions that will impact your growth and give your spirit the enterprising touch it needs to reach its fullest glory.

In the translation of *The Upanishads*, Eknath Easwaran says: "Dare like a teenager — reach for the highest you can conceive, with everything you have, and never count the cost." The biggest decisions need an element of risk, an element of buccaneering. When the Tatas bought Corus Steel, there was the Damoclean sword of the probable market repercussions looming over their head. But then they surged forward boldly, with the assurance that the tide will turn in their favour. And turn it did. As they say: "Luck favours the brave." People who have discovered new territories, those who have forged new ground, leaders who have blazed new trails and frontrunners who have found new vistas have all had courage. They have stretched themselves out of the straightjacket of anxiety and paranoia into the wonderland of courage and dominion.

Courage is a quality that must come from within. If it comes from external sources, then it is just an assurance, which is momentary. Give yourself a daily dose of courage. Talk to yourself. Tell yourself that you are bold, brave and confident. A fearless person listens always to the voice of conscience and not to the noises of people around him.

Courage is the most exalted state of being. Countless people over the ages have sacrificed their lives to uphold this state. They have done it so that one day all of us can live free of fear in an ideal society. People who have done the most good to humankind (Mahatma Gandhi, Nelson Mandela, Martin Luthur King, Mother Teresa, to name a very few) are the ones who are the most fearless. They are afraid neither of persecution nor of ridicule, neither of slander nor of brickbats. To them, the only life worthy of living is a life of absolute freedom. As Dada Vaswani once said: "I would be free or not be at all!" True freedom can be claimed only by courage. It can be preserved only by courage. And it can be granted only by courage. With courage by your side, you can accomplish the biggest feat and conquer the most menacing evils. You will no longer live a petty life governed by trivial thoughts. You will inhabit the kingdom of miracles and become an upholder of the highest ideals that humankind espouses. As someone has said: "Courage is not a gift, it is a decision." Make that decision now, and reap the benefits forevermore.

12

Be a Constant Learner

A Chinese proverb says: "To be fond of learning is to be at the gate of knowledge." An interested student meets the teacher more than halfway — all the way, if necessary. Learning is the best way to stretch oneself. There is veritably so much to learn that it can never be enough. Pick up a book, start a course, switch on the TV, get on to Google, talk to someone, and there is something new to assimilate always.

With most people, the learning curve ends in school or college. And even there, it's mostly by rote. I will again share with you a personal example: In my spare time as a model, I thought it'd be insightful to learn about numerology. For six months, I read many books and surfed the Net extensively to learn about the subject. The good point of it was that I gradually took to it so well that I wrote a book on numerology, *God Speaks in Numbers*, and even started contributing a column called Number Nirvana to the erstwhile *Today* newspaper. Today, thanks to numerology, I have been introduced to some of the most fascinating people I otherwise might have never met.

What I'm trying to say here is that even if there is no direct incentive to learn, plunge yourself into a new subject, and you never know what priceless nugget might come your way!

Apart from change, let the only constant in your life be learning. Only by learning a lesson and implementing it will you go to the next level, will you evolve. Endeavour to learn, not just about fields that directly affect you but about a wider gamut of fields. And don't equate learning with mugging up. Learning doesn't require you to be a collector of facts. For that you have the encyclopedia, the newspaper and the Internet. Learning is a much more profound process that affects you at a very fundamental, intrinsic level. It is a tool that ushers a transformation in the very way you look at things and express yourself.

Learning is not just about fields — it's about life, about the unique experiences and challenges we all are constantly presented with. As Dada Vaswani has said: "You must keep learning. Every new day comes to us as a new opportunity from the hands of the Spotless One. Each day holds the promise that we can renew our life at any time and at any stage. All that you need is the mood of a student. Be a student all your life." Keep emptying your cups of knowledge so that you can keep filling it up ever so often. But if the cup is overflowing with conceit and wilfulness, how will you put any more in it? In the Western world, there are many people who've been known to join universities even at the age of 70 or so! We all need to have that keenness and willing spirit for an enriching life. After *Rab Ne Bana Di Jodi* released, Shahrukh Khan, a veteran of 20 years and 60-plus films, had this to say about the debutante Anushka Sharma: "When I worked with Anushka, it made me realise that there is a whole new world of enacting a scene. People think that I guided her. Rather, she is the one who, without knowing, has directed me in the film. I learnt so much from her. I thank her for teaching me how to act in a different way and for making my film so beautiful." What a tremendous approach to learning!

And the best part about learning is that it is not the preserve of a select few, nor is it constricted by age, wealth or creed. The only determinant is personal choice and free will. We all know of ample instances when those with advanced formal education fare averagely while those with very basic formal education surpass and outshine everybody. The reason is that the latter educate themselves in the real sense of the word. They learn what has to be learnt, whether on the job or from those in the know. They are the biggest exponents of self-study and their lives attest to the fact that true education cannot be given, it can only be had; it can never be deprived, it can only be willed; it can never limit, it can only liberate. So keep learning, and open the doors to a beautiful today and an even more glorious tomorrow.

13

Keep the Child in You Alive

Enthusiasm is the most desirable state of being. It infuses you with vigour and marks your life with dynamism. In fact, one can learn this quality best from children. Just notice how children behave. Even if they are watching TV or drinking a glass of water — or even if they are not doing anything — they are very enthusiastic. Their approach to even the most "mundane" things is so bright and energetic! While it is perfectly understandable that you might not wish to inculcate a similar juvenile enthusiasm, yet it is very important to keep the child in you alive. In the throes of adulthood, if you can retain the effervescence of childhood, it is the most ideal balance. By being enthusiastic, you can lift the spirit of all those around you. Your joie de vivre can elevate everyone. The quality of playfulness is very important in life. Most people tend to become stiff and serious, and they associate maturity with gravity. But actually the opposite is true. This is what I read about a yogi once: "In the midst of children, he has the special talent to become a child, and in the midst of adults, he has the special talent to make them feel like children again!" This is the state we should all aspire towards.

By increasing your enthusiasm, you announce to the universe that you're going to play your part as graciously as you can. Most people look and behave like zombies, lacklustre and with zero enthusiasm to life and work. They are very mechanical and sterile in their approach. Abiding enthusiasm comes when you are determined to enjoy your life, no matter what. Everybody loves to be around enthusiastic, happy people. I feel that the best gift you can give anyone is to make them happy. By being enthusiastic, you'd be happy not just yourself but you'd make others happy too. People at the forefront of their vocations are those who are deeply enthusiastic about what they do. Shahrukh Khan once said: "To me, going to the sets every day is a pleasure. The day it becomes a chore, I'd quit!" I read it more than a decade ago, and ever since he's gone only from strength to strength. Just goes to show that the more enthusiastic he's been, the more successful he's been, and vice versa. Enthusiasm makes work look not like a chore, but a pleasure; it makes life seem not lacklustre, but lustrous; it makes work seem not mundane, but fun. So be enthusiastic and invite others to join you in this revelation called life — you have no idea how much fun it can be!

14

Never Retire

It's shocking when you sometimes meet people who talk of going into government white-collar jobs, because, "when you retire, you get a good pension!" It sounds funny, but it really is unfortunate. Imagine, they are willing to trade their lives for a pension cheque, which they'd receive after sloughing at a non-gratifying job for 35–40 years! On the contrary, if you look at business leaders all over the world, they have a tireless, voracious appetite for their life and work. The thought of retiring doesn't even occur to them. And why should it? The thought of retiring oneself, like all other thoughts, is self-fulfilling. It conditions the mind and body to function only upto the point one has mentally set. If you look at Bollywood actors, most of the top ones are in their mid to late forties. Just take a leaf from their book. In an industry governed by the so-called diktats of age, they are all reigning supreme. They've proven that, if you're willing to do something, nothing can deter you — not age, not circumstances, nothing at all. It is imperative that you keep at it. Stay focused. I read this beautiful line somewhere long ago: "Light is innocuous when scattered. But when concentrated, it acquires the intensity of a laser beam that can pierce through the sharpest diamonds and the strongest iron vaults." How true! Even if you have to mandatorily give up something at a certain age — let's say a job, where your services will be terminated as a matter of policy — accept it gracefully and start something afresh. Begin a new innings, herald a new chapter. Probably you have been doing a managerial desk job all your life, and you always deeply wanted to start a garden-landscaping outfit. Why not do it now? Probably, you were a field executive, and you wanted to devote more time to writing. Why not do it now? Probably, you were a banker, and you wanted to open a crèche. Why not do it now? There are tons of opportunities waiting to be seized. But for that, you have to get out of the retirement mode and spur yourself to greater heights. No matter how much you have achieved or done, there's always more that you can still do. The very purpose of human existence is to ceaselessly work towards ever-greater heights and glory. There is so much potential yet untapped, so much energy yet unharnessed.

Life is too important for regrets. Every moment holds an opportunity for us to live our dream, create a new one or to make amends, if needed. Please don't commit the mistake of rationing your life in years — a folly most people in their fifties and sixties commit: "Oh, what to do now! We've lived our life. As for the balance 20–30 years, those too will pass!" Imagine, if God were to think your life has served its purpose, then why would he let you live any longer! The very fact that you are on this planet — whether you are 1 or 100 — means that your mission is still not over, that God wants you to see and do more than you already have. Use that time, not cringing in resignation, but in enjoying the fullest glory of this beautiful condition called human life.

15

Be Inspired

I once read somewhere: "In life, people stronger and happier than you often cross your path. When you see or hear about such people, don't be jealous. God has planted them your way to encourage you." What an amazing way to stretch jealousy into inspiration!

I have always admired polymaths — people who are versatile and can put several irons in the fire simultaneously. I personally consider Leonardo da Vinci to be a huge inspiration on me. Whenever I'd read about him, I'd get very inspired. He had 11 professions, and he excelled in all of them! I'd constantly tell myself that one day I have to be as versatile too. As I said earlier, I've had till date 12 professions. Though I must honestly admit that I'm nowhere even remotely close to his stature or depth in any of them, yet I have at least managed to be touched by the essence of these, and I'm today a very happy person for it. Every person who is a success has to have a source of inspiration, be it a person, a fictitious character, a motto or something in nature. It's not important who or what your source of inspiration is but rather how much you get inspired from it. If you keep a quote mug or sticker in your room, even that can be an enormous inspiration, so long as you absorb the message intently. Having a role model can be a worthy stimulant too. Warren Buffet once said of his two mentors: "I'm 15 per cent Philip Fisher and 85 per cent Benjamin Graham!" Napoleon Hill once suggested that our ultimate aim should be to be great ourselves, but till then, the next best thing is to emulate great people, by feeling and acting, as nearly as possible. Like, let's say, somebody who wants to do action comedy might be inspired by Jackie Chan or if someone wants to be a music composer, they might be inspired by AR Rahman. In my case, it is Shahrukh Khan — I've found his success, or rather his life, so inspiring that I look forward every time to reading his interviews and emulating his example in my work and life.

In order to be inspired, you need two things: First of all, be willing. And, second, seek inspiration actively. Even a painting, a photograph or a sculpture can inspire you. To a heightened person, the source is immaterial. Inspiration is all around us: nature, children, birds, animals, still-life objects, art, books, our friends, family, everywhere. All we need is a willing heart, keen eyes and an open mind. Also, one has to sublimate the ego to let inspiration touch oneself. Even if you're the best at your craft, there is more that you can still learn, even from a newcomer. You've probably lost enthusiasm in your quest for excellence and a fresh rookie might have lots of it. So you can get inspired regardless of your stature and station in life. In fact, the higher you go, the more inspiration you need. Just like the higher you scale a mountain, the more oxygen you need. And the beauty about inspiration, like in life, is: to each their own. Each one of us has to choose our own source. What works for one might not work for the other and vice versa. And it's not like you have to be fixated on one person or source. At any moment, any person or thing or experience might inspire you. Don't block yourself from the revelation. Rather, embrace it wholeheartedly. I've seen that people who themselves are the most inspired, in turn inspire others the most and make life so much more meaningful for everybody.

16

Respect Thyself

Self-respect is the cornerstone of a fulfilled life. It is the ingredient that governs how others will eventually perceive you. It is imperative that you respect yourself before others respect you. It's quite like saying if you don't keep your house clean, others will not come to do it for you. Or if you don't groom yourself, a passerby will not do it. Likewise with self-respect. If you don't respect yourself, others will not either.

It honestly doesn't take much to respect, like or love yourself. One of the most dynamic people I've ever met had this to say about himself: "I have been living with myself for 42 years. I love myself so much that I feel like hugging myself sometimes!" What an attitude! And honestly, knowing him, I can vouchsafe that there was not a shred of narcissism or vanity in what he was saying. Rather, he said this with moist eyes and a spiritual profoundness. One of the most beautiful chants in Sanskrit is "Aham Brahma Asmi" or "Whatever God is, I am". Read it again: "WHATEVER GOD IS, I AM." Imagine, God is not outside, but inside! We keep vainly looking for him outside, in idols, in scriptures, in places of worship. But he's actually inside you. So just like you respect a temple, shouldn't you also respect your inner self — the true residence of God!

To give you an example: two siblings raised in the very same house, in the very same set of circumstances, don't quite rise to the same level. What's the reason? The one who rises invariably has a heightened sense of self-worth and wants to evolve, while the other has low self-esteem and becomes a driftwood, going whichever way the current takes them. The inference is clear: those who excel have a very high self-esteem and those who don't have low regard for themselves. See yourself as priceless, and you will always have high self-respect. Always remember that how others see you is directly proportional with how you see yourself. If your self-image is warped, others will be wary of you. Continually feed yourself with the best thoughts, words, feelings and experiences. Talk to yourself in the loveliest way possible. Auto-suggest your way to your dream life. Tell yourself, "I'm capable", "I'm healthy", I'm loved", "I'm at peace", "I'm amazing", "I'm the best" with vigour as many times as you can. When you look at yourself in the mirror, regardless of how good or not-so-good you look, don't self-deprecate. Rather behold yourself with tenderness and affection. Say some nice words to your reflection: "Hey, wow you look so beautiful!" "Hey, who's that handsome dude!" You'll instantly feel more charged and positive. Always remember that *you* are all that you actually have. If *you* don't give yourself respect, then who will you give it to, and who will give you respect in turn? Paulo Coelho once said: "Every gesture made by a human being is sacred, and full of consequences." So, treat yourself like a VVVIP and others will follow suit. Joel

Osteen once beautifully said: "Just like a hundred-dollar bill has the same value — whether it's fresh from the mint or it has aged and is all crumpled and soiled — we do too! In fact, we will never, ever lose our value. Our value has been placed in us by the creator of the universe, and nobody can take it away from us." So, my friend, respect yourself and cherish the incalculable value God has placed in you.

17

Turn Stones into Milestones

There is a saying: "Difficulty is the nurse of greatness!" Every limitation brings with it the seed of opportunity. People who have excelled all over the world are the ones who have surpassed hurdles and obstacles. The *Forbes* magazine, while presenting its 2008 annual rich list, had this to say: "Two thirds of the world's billionaires have made their fortunes from scratch, relying on grit and determination, and not good genes!" Let's see how: Russia's richest man, Roman Abramovich, was an orphan. Apple's Steve Jobs was adopted. He dropped out of college when he couldn't pay the tuition. Oprah Winfrey became a mother at 14 and her child passed away after birth. The world's wealthiest novelist, JK Rowling, was unemployed, on welfare and a single mother.

Limitations are there in every person's life. But the ones who excel are those that surpass those limitations. If Beethoven, despite being deaf, could compose some of the greatest musical compositions ever, then there's no reason why any of us can't excel in our chosen fields of activity! Helen Keller's is the ultimate example of overcoming hurdles: she had virtual every impairment any human being can ever have, yet by dint of her determination, she left an indelible mark on humanity. Talking of physical hurdles, there are scores of people all over the world who are running marathons despite loosing their feet to calamities. Stephen Hawking, despite being severely disabled by motor neuron disease, has gone on to be one of the greatest physicists ever. Franklin D Roosevelt, one of the most legendary American presidents ever, served his entire tenure from the wheelchair. Tom Cruise overcame dyslexia and a 5'7" frame to become one of the greatest movie stars in the world. Sylvester Stallone battled poverty and severe physical ailments as a child to be one of the highest paid Hollywood actors. When Arnold Schwarzenegger came to America at the age of 21, he didn't know a word of English, but he became not just a megastar but also the governor of California. Amitabh Bachchan overcame asthma to become a superstar. Wasim Akram, who became a diabetic at the prime of his career, took 250 wickets after contracting the disease. Sean Connery was a milk-delivery man and a coffin maker who went on to be James Bond. Meryl Streep was a waitress who went to be an Oscar winner. Rajnikanth was a bus conductor; Akshay Kumar a waiter. Mithun Chakraborty was so poor that he did not have money even to go to Delhi to collect the National Award in acting for his first film. At the age of 21, doctors had diagnosed Hrithik Roshan with scoliosis and told him that he could never be an actor — he went on to overcome not just that but also stammering, a vestigial thumb and a scrawny physique to become one of the greatest movie icons India has ever seen. BS Chandrashekhar was afflicted with polio but went on to become one of the greatest spin bowlers in the world.

Thomas Alva Edison had only three months of schooling in his life, yet he became one of the greatest inventors ever. Similarly, there are countless others who, through their grit and determination, have turned limitations into landmarks, and given the world a worthy precedent to follow.

The Chinese character for crisis combines two seemingly conflicting symbols: one for danger, the other for opportunity! Just goes to show how inseparable the two are. Opportunities in life often come incognito. Today, as I look back on my own life, I have grown the most in life when I've had to surmount the biggest obstacles. Everything in the universe happens for a reason, even if on the face of it, it seems totally baffling and incomprehensible. When faced with obstacles, don't turn away. Sometimes all you need to do is to look them in the face and go right through them. Just like gold cannot become pure without being burnished and diamond cannot become spectacular without friction, no human being can progress without obstacles. So rise up and surmount them. You'll be amazed at what you will become. On breaking the world record for the highest Test runs, Sachin Tendulkar memorably said: "There are stones thrown at you, and you turn them into milestones." So, come rain or sun, take everything in your stride and keep turning your trials into your triumphs and your stones into your milestones.

18

Celebrate Life

In the acknowledgements page of my short stories book, *And the Show Goes On*, I wrote what I think are the best words I have ever written: "To life, the greatest blessing of all!" I think we live in the best time ever in humanity, when there is a phenomenal multitude of choices: if one seeks entertainment, there are mind-boggling options; if one wants to shop, there are haberdashers and high-street designer malls alike; if one wants to work, never before has an environment been more conducive and adaptive to newer ideas and capitalist ventures; if one wants to travel, there are innovative destinations and modes of travel. There is so much happening all around that it's a sheer blessing to be alive.

As Bob Proctor has said: "Enjoy life, because life is phenomenal. It's a magnificent trip!" Lucky are those who celebrate every moment, every day of their lives, and that too without reason! Imagine, what is the most important thing in life? Put yourself through a small experiment: Hold your breath for as long as you can. Push yourself to the furthest limit, to as far as you can go and then some more, to the point where you start gasping. Now release and inhale. How long could you live in this condition? 30 seconds? 1 minute? Max 2 minutes? Now imagine all the other things that you have: food, water, house, clothes, cars, money, office, gadgets, etc. If not more, you could live without any or all of these for at least 2–3 days. The stronger among us can manage even longer. Now that's how important our breath is? So if you are one of those who complain that there is nothing else in your life to celebrate, then why not celebrate your breath, the very essence of your life! And once you start celebrating on such a basic level, all the other levels — physical, mental, material — will become pure celebration too.

My favourite piece of wisdom is from a Smirnoff commercial: "Life is calling. Where are you?" Actually, life is calling out to us every instant. But are we responding to its call? Approach every day with a festive spirit, as if it's Diwali, Gurpurab, Eid or Christmas. Be grateful for being alive, and make a resolve to feast yourself in this banquet of life. Most people continually look for "reasons" to be happy, for occasions to rejoice. Is it not reason enough to be *alive*? Is it not occasion enough to celebrate our existence on this wonderful planet where the miracle of life is unfolding every instant for billions of human beings, apart from countless other life forms? Is the rising of the sun every day not a splendour enough? Is the colour of the sky not reason enough to make us erupt into euphoria? Is the fragrance of flowers not incentive enough to love life? And if you're one of the lucky ones to receive the blessings of a wonderful family, then are you not truly blessed? Is having a family in itself not a reason to celebrate? Why should you look for once-a-year occasions like anniversaries and birthdays to reach out and celebrate? Why not a spontaneous, instant, non-occasional celebration? When you actually look at life itself as a celebration, then, trust me, life will give you many more reasons for celebration. That's a guarantee.

Anthony D'Angelo once beautifully said: "Life is meant to be enjoyed, not endured!" By all means work towards what you don't have but enjoy what you have. True celebration is inside you. Once you find it there, the outside is but a reflection. As someone has said: "Celebrate life, and life will celebrate you back." So go ahead and celebrate life — it's the biggest high there is ever going to be!

About the Author

After doing a book-publishing course from the University of Denver, Colorado, Vickrant Mahajan joined HarperCollins Publishers in New Delhi in 2001 as a manuscript editor. In 2003, he became the First runner-up and Mr Photogenic at Grasim Mr India, and his life changed forever. Change, in fact, has been the only constant in Vickrant's life! He has segued between twelve different professions — as an author, editor, publisher, photographer, model, actor, numerologist, voice-over artist, communication trainer, columnist, scriptwriter, motivator — and he has enjoyed each one of them thoroughly. His first three books, *Model Dreams, Shooting from the Lip, God Speaks in Numbers*, were non-fiction works, while his fourth, *And the Show Goes On*, was a collection of short stories. Besides, he has compiled his wife's coffee-table book, *The Eye of Eternity*, authored four privately commissioned photographic coffee-table books, *A Royal Saga, Lageen, My Red-Letter Day, Stunning!* and has exhibited his photographs in India and Dubai. *Stretch Yourself* is his tenth book. He is married to lifestyle photographer Ronicka Kandhari and lives in New Delhi.